THIS BOOK BELONGS TO

ONE WORD

FOR TODAY

FOR SPIRIT-FILLED LIVING

A 90-DAY DEVOTIONAL

Chosen
a division of Baker Publishing Group
Minneapolis, Minnesota

© 2021 by Baker Publishing Group

Published by Chosen Books
11400 Hampshire Avenue South
Bloomington, Minnesota 55438
www.chosenbooks.com

Chosen Books is a division of
Baker Publishing Group, Grand Rapids, Michigan

Printed in China

Library of Congress Cataloging-in-Publication Data
Title: One word for today for spirit-filled living : a 90-day devotional.
Description: Minneapolis, Minnesota : Chosen Books, a division of Baker Publishing
    Group, [2021] | Includes bibliographical references.
Identifiers: LCCN 2021014167 | ISBN 9780800762308 (cloth) | ISBN 9781493433490
    (ebook)
Subjects: LCSH: Devotional literature.
Classification: LCC BV4832.3 .O54 2021 | DDC 242/.2—dc23
LC record available at https://lccn.loc.gov/2021014167

Written by Gretchen Rodriguez and David Sluka

Cover design by Studio Gearbox

21   22   23   24   25   26   27   7   6   5   4   3   2   1

CONTENTS

INTRODUCTION

The Word of God is powerful and sharper than any sword, and meditating upon it has renewed the mind and transformed the human soul for thousands of years. The Holy Spirit makes the Word come alive so that it directs, comforts, reveals and heals.

With so much potential in these God-breathed words, shouldn't we give them more attention? Yet sometimes, in the midst of busyness and distraction, pressures and conflict, you may struggle or fail to notice that God is present with you in every moment.

The content of this book will be like an anchor for your busy mind. Each day you will focus on one word that will guide your attention toward the Lord in the context of the biblical theme for that day. As you lean into Him, thoughtfully reading and meditating, the presence of the Holy Spirit will meet you.

Throughout the day, as the Spirit reminds you of the daily word, ask Him for greater insight. Receive His strength. And look for an opportunity to put that word into practice. You may be surprised how appropriate each word is for that day.

The two short pages of each day's reading contain the following:

- Your daily word
- The Scripture that inspired that day's word—read it purposefully and prayerfully
- An inspirational meditation that you can read in under two minutes
- A personalized reflective question and prayer to help you process, with the Holy Spirit, what you have read
- An affirmative declaration and practical action to activate the word with the Lord's help

Each day's reading, while short, is not a quick snack, but a meal to savor throughout your day. Post the word in a prominent place. Consider repeating or memorizing the Scripture and declaration of faith. You may want to set a few alarms throughout the day to quicken your memory of the word and to declare the short truth. You will discover that your meditation will bring nourishment.

May this book bless you and bolster your faith as you focus on one word from the Lord and set your mind on things above. Most importantly, may you discover an even deeper relationship with the One who cares for you and guides you with His everlasting love.

1 | SHINE

> "Don't hide your light! Let it shine brightly before others, so that your commendable works will shine as light upon them, and then they will give their praise to your Father in heaven."
>
> Matthew 5:16 TPT

Jesus wants you to *let* your light shine. Have you ever been tempted to dim or hide His light?

Hindrances that get in the way of shining God's pure light include not wanting to be proud or draw undue attention to yourself, and not knowing or discounting your true potential in Christ. Shame and fear of rejection are also tools the enemy uses to keep you in the dark.

Jesus said shining draws attention to the *Father*. So shine brightly as you rest in the humility of Christ. Light can bring welcome illumination, but it can also be a startling interruption for those comfortable in darkness. No matter the response you receive from others, God wants you to shine.

There are many ways to shine. Share a gift or talent He has given to you, be a person of excellence, tell someone what God has done in your life or serve behind the scenes unto the Lord. Letting the Holy Spirit shine the brilliant light of Christ through you is to be who God has created you to be. Fight the temptation to turn down the intensity of His radiance.

Your light is bright, so let yourself shine!

REFLECT What may be keeping the light of Jesus from shining at full strength in my life?

PRAY Jesus, Light of the World, forgive me for hiding or dimming Your light in any way. Make Your face shine upon me and give me courage to shine brightly at home and at work, personally and professionally, with who I am in You and what I do for You. I want my life to inspire others to praise You.

DECLARE Jesus shines through me to influence my world.

ACT Ask the Holy Spirit to show you one person or situation He wants to shine on through you today, then follow His leading.

God is our merciful Father and the source of all comfort. He comforts us in all our troubles so that we can comfort others. When they are troubled, we will be able to give them the same comfort God has given us.

2 Corinthians 1:3–4 NLT

God is not opposed to comfort. He is the Source of all comfort. But there is a difference between being comforted and being comfortable.

God does not want us to chase comfort or—like the Israelites—beg to go back to "Egypt" because the road to walking in God's promises is filled with difficulty. Being comfortable should not be our pursuit, but rather enjoying communion with our Comforter and Helper—the Holy Spirit with you and in you.

Where do you go when you need comfort? You can seek and find comfort apart from God and find yourself in unhealthy addictions. Or you can cry out to God, knowing He hears you and will answer.

How has God comforted you in the past? When you comfort another person with the comfort God has given to you, God turns for good what the enemy meant for evil. This is one way "God causes everything to work together for the good of those who love God and are called according to his purpose" (Romans 8:28 NLT).

The Holy Spirit is your Comforter today. Receive what you need from Him, and when the time is right, share that comfort with others.

REFLECT What do I do—or where do I go—when I need comfort?

PRAY Pray God of All Comfort, You are the source of the comfort I need. You heal me when I am broken, and You are merciful when I am in trouble. Forgive me for running to people, places or things for comfort instead of seeking You to satisfy my desires. Draw near to me, make me whole and empower me to release Your comfort to those around me.

DECLARE The Holy Spirit comforts me.

ACT Reach out to comfort someone today with the comfort God has given to you.

3 | GOODNESS

Surely goodness and mercy shall follow me all the days of my life: and I will dwell in the house of the LORD for ever.

Psalm 23:6 KJV

What does it look like to have God's goodness following you? Not just following you on a good day, but every day of your life?

You may be familiar with God's *hand* of blessing upon you. But as you meditate on His goodness, you will discover an even deeper revelation—there is only One who *is* good (see Matthew 19:17).

Goodness is the core quality of God's nature. He cannot not be good. In the same way you can expect fruit from a fruit tree, you can expect goodness from God. Wherever you see goodness in your life, it is a gift from God. "Whatever is good and perfect is a gift coming down . . . from God our Father" (James 1:17 NLT). Goodness in the world is a gift from God, often expressed through those made in His image.

God's goodness that He has stored up for you is abundant. Because God is with you, you can expect goodness to follow you every day. Today, let the promise of God's goodness awaken expectancy and be your anchor in troubling times. Instead of rehearsing what is going wrong, remind yourself that God is working all things out for your good.

REFLECT What does my day look like today? Am I expecting God's goodness?

PRAY Good Father, everything good I have and every good thing I experience comes from You. Thank You for the way You unceasingly care for me. You are generous, compassionate and kind. Throughout the day, help me to notice Your many blessings. From the moment I wake until I lay my head down to rest, I will focus on Your immeasurable goodness and praise You.

DECLARE God's goodness follows me wherever I go.

ACT Notice and record in some way the goodness of God you see today.

4 | BELIEVE

"Blessed are those who believe without seeing me."

John 20:29 NLT

Have you ever felt that believing would be easier if you could see Jesus with your physical eyes? Thankfully, Jesus promised great blessings to those who believe in their hearts without seeing Him with their eyes.

Every day we are either led by the sights around us or guided by the Kingdom of God within us. If we're not mindful of these ever-competing forces fighting for our loyalties, we may easily succumb to unbelief. Belief does not have to be based on what we see, but on the reality of our relationship with God, "for we live by believing and not by seeing" (2 Corinthians 5:7 NLT)

Belief cannot be forced. Our belief in God grows and becomes firmly grounded the more we know and experience God. We then believe when we do not see because we trust He is on our side and is working all things out for our good (see Romans 8:28).

Many people in Jesus' day saw Him but did not believe in Him. Today, where you are struggling with doubt, recall the good work God has done in your life. Let His presence strengthen your belief again.

REFLECT How hard is it for me to believe without seeing?

PRAY Lord Jesus, help my unbelief and forgive me when I trust only in what I can see with my physical eyes. Pour out Your grace and love as I choose to believe in the finished work of Your Son, Jesus, and the ongoing work of the Holy Spirit in my life. You are faithful and trustworthy. Open my spiritual eyes to see what my natural eyes cannot.

DECLARE I believe in Jesus, no matter what I see.

ACT Recall how God has shown Himself to you, in big and small ways. Your belief in God rests on a solid foundation of His Word and His work in your life.

> So when the LORD saw that he turned aside to look, God called to him from the midst of the bush and said, "Moses, Moses!" And he said, "Here I am."
>
> Exodus 3:4 NKJV

God is wild about you! And throughout the day, He repeatedly and graciously tries to capture your attention.

Every morning, our Father reaches out with kindness and mercy, a gentle wooing of our hearts that we either acknowledge or ignore. Each day, He calls us to turn aside to hear from heaven so that we may know His heart. He invites us to come closer, where hidden gems of wisdom, love, revelation and communion are found.

Like He did for Moses, God sets things in our path to get our attention—a sunrise, a stranger, an email, a conversation, or a random thought. He draws us in unlimited ways. But how we respond is up to us. When Moses saw the burning bush, he stopped, turned to look, and when God spoke, he replied with a heart fully intent on receiving whatever God offered.

Today, this magnificent and awe-inspiring God, the One whose voice sparks a fire and whose gentle whispers carry on the wind, is drawing you closer because He loves you. Don't rush through the day, oblivious to the ways He is speaking, teaching and loving you. The answer you need may be right in front of you.

REFLECT What is God doing in my life that gives me the opportunity to draw closer to Him?

PRAY Father God, I feel Your lovingkindness drawing me closer. Thank You for reminding me that You are longing for more than a casual glance; You're looking for my undivided heart. So that is what I give You—all of me, without reservation. Speak, Lord, I'm listening. Here I am. I am Yours.

DECLARE God is drawing me closer. I am moving closer to Him.

ACT Take a few moments to turn aside and take a closer look at something God is showing you.

> You will keep him in perfect peace, whose mind is
> stayed on You, because he trusts in You.
>
> Isaiah 26:3 NKJV

What would it be like to experience peace every day?
Not bumping into it occasionally, but abiding in perfect
peace, constantly.

At this very moment, the Prince of Peace is with
you. Not only with you, but in you, around you, wrap-
ping you in a blanket of serenity that surpasses understanding. But unless you recognize this incredible blessing, you will likely miss it. Peace is a gift, but one you
must reach out to receive.

Receiving and walking in peace means choosing to
release the cares of this world that easily entangle your
soul. It is a heavenly exchange—your stress for Jesus'
peace. Take your hands off the situations you cannot
control and ask the Lord to take over.

You will not experience the peace you desper-
ately crave if you are busy trying to fix everything and
everyone. A quiet, trusting heart starts with a mind
focused on God. Ponder Him continually. Refuse the

temptation to fear, and if you notice anxiety creeping in, set your mind on the love, power and faithfulness of your Father in heaven.

Keep this promise from Isaiah in your thoughts today. The Lord longs to bless you with perfect peace.

REFLECT When was the last time I experienced God's perfect peace?

PRAY Jesus, my Prince of Peace, I give to You all my worries and obsessive thoughts. You care about the things on my heart, and You have the answer for each one. Today, I reject fearful imaginations and set my mind on You. Pour out Your peace and guide me, today, with a heart at rest in You.

DECLARE I have peace because my mind is focused on God and trusts in Him.

ACT Write down on a piece of paper the name of whatever is producing unrest in your life. Symbolically lift it to the Lord. Then in bold letters write *PERFECT PEACE* over what you have written.

7 | PERSPECTIVE

> We don't focus our attention on what is seen but on what is unseen. For what is seen is temporary, but the unseen realm is eternal.
>
> 2 Corinthians 4:18 TPT

The way you interpret situations will lead to faith or fear. This is why it is vital to immediately get God's perspective on everything that comes your way.

God does not see things the way we do. His wisdom is far greater. He has a perfect vantage point. Fear does not skew or block His view, and He wants to share His perspective with us. We need the mind of Christ.

Rational thinking isn't God's way of thinking. Quite often, the stance of faith is contrary to what makes sense in the natural. When we see a blocked path, God sees a way that leads to something better. Unless we step back and ask for His guidance, we may miss it. When something irritates us and tempts us to react, the Spirit of God wants to soften our hearts and show us how to pray. With every opposition, God will release His wisdom and peace if we focus our attention on Him and become heavenly minded.

So, today, regardless of what happens, take a deep breath and find His presence. Ask for His perspective, and as you fix your heart on Him, you will discover it.

REFLECT How often do I react to a person or situation instead of seeking God's perspective?

PRAY All-Knowing God, forgive me for analyzing situations that cannot be understood without Your insight. I need Your wisdom. I ask for Your perspective. As I fix my mind on You, give me eyes to see what You are doing and ears to hear what You are saying. In the heights of Your glorious presence, You will show me the way.

DECLARE God helps me see from His perspective.

ACT Pause and ask God to show you how He sees something in your life that needs a fresh point of view. Then adjust your response accordingly.

8 | LISTEN

Then the voice of God thundered from within the cloud, "This is my Son, my Beloved One. Listen carefully to all he has to say."

Luke 9:35 TPT

What do you do more in your relationship with God: talk or listen? God longs to speak to you, His child, and share secrets reserved only for you.

There is nothing as healing and calming as the sweetness of God's voice. There is nothing more reviving and faith building than the power of His roar. God warmly invites us to be with Him—to step away from the noise of life and soul and cultivate a listening heart.

To do this, we position ourselves by getting quiet. Without uttering a word, we set our affection on the Lord and wait. Sometimes He'll remind us of a Scripture, show us a picture or speak tenderly to the heart. Other times, we may only *feel* His love, then later, to our surprise, He speaks through His creation, a friend or something we read.

Yes, at times, you may petition, vent or intercede. God loves to listen when you speak to Him. But the

Holy Spirit also wants to show you what is on His heart.

The Father wants to reveal Jesus, His Beloved One, to you. Today, esteem and prioritize His voice more than your own and listen carefully to all He has to say.

REFLECT What is the last thing God has spoken to me (through the Bible, a person, an impression from the Holy Spirit or another means)?

PRAY Attentive Father, I accept this invitation to cultivate a listening heart. I want to know You—to be ushered into a new level of fellowship by having a quiet and attentive spirit. Holy Spirit, teach me to tune in to You, as I esteem Your voice more vital than my eloquent prayers. I am empowered by all You say.

DECLARE I listen carefully to all God has to say to me.

ACT During your prayer time today, just listen.

9 | BEHOLD

> One thing I have desired of the LORD, that will I seek:
> That I may dwell in the house of the LORD all the
> days of my life, to behold the beauty of the LORD,
> and to inquire in His temple.
>
> Psalm 27:4 NKJV

Have you noticed that what you focus on affects how you think and feel? Starting the day with one desire can often play a predominant role in how you approach the day.

When the "one thing" you desire is to remain aware of the Lord, He will be what you continuously return to when problems arise or distractions come. When His face fills your vision, other preoccupations fade away. You can cultivate a peaceful perspective by beholding Him in the quiet of your heart. Gazing at Him reminds you of His love, faithfulness and provision. It is difficult to feel overwhelmed when He is all you see. His presence sheds light on the darkest places.

Today you have the choice to fixate on problems or behold the One who holds the answers. See His eyes blazing with love for you. Stand in awe of His perfect wisdom. He knows what is on your heart, and He knows how to walk you through it.

But first, release those cares into His hands. Let nothing skew your vision. Come closer and behold Him in His magnificence. Let His beauty, His love and the privilege of coming before the Creator capture your heart today.

REFLECT What gets most of my attention each day?

PRAY Precious Jesus, wash my mind with peace as I turn my gaze to You. Regardless of what the day holds, I will keep my heart before You. And when distractions come, I will step back and quiet my soul in Your presence. Beholding You will enable me to see things rightly—through the glory of Your love.

DECLARE I behold Jesus and desire Him most.

ACT Shut down every distraction for a few minutes and behold Jesus and the beauty of His creation in your thoughts.

10 | HOPE

"For I know the plans I have for you," declares the
LORD, "plans to prosper you and not to harm you,
plans to give you hope and a future."

Jeremiah 29:11 NIV

Hope is not something you can fake. But hope can be
birthed through the power of God's Word.

The Lord knows our frailty and tendency to feel
overwhelmed. He knows that we sometimes fall prey to
weariness, which is why He has woven encouragement
throughout His Word. God wants us to remember that
we have His attention. Our loving Father is thinking
about us, longing for us to believe that He has good
things in store for us. He wants us to hold Scriptures like
Jeremiah 29:11 close to our hearts during trying times.

God has promised us a future filled with hope. No
matter what we face, regardless of the trials and pain,
He is able to turn things around. Nothing is impossible
for Him! Instead of recounting our troubles and talking
about them day after day, we can spotlight God's promises and soak in His love. Let's dive into His Word and
saturate ourselves with hope and faith.

When you focus on God's goodness and frequently remind yourself of His promises, heaviness falls away. When you are drenched in His presence, His Word uproots lies you have believed. God has new hope for you today.

✺ **REFLECT** What area of my life needs a boost of hope today?

✺ **PRAY** God of Hope, thank You for the hope You provide. You are good, and Your faithfulness has been proven time after time. Forgive me for partnering with discouragement and fear. I feel the winds of hope reviving me again. Your Word releases light and life. Your nearness makes it easy to believe. I place my hope in You alone.

✺ **DECLARE** Hope is rising because I know God has plans to prosper me.

✺ **ACT** In an area you have felt hopeless, declare the promise of Jeremiah 29:11.

11 | BLESS

> Bless the LORD, O my soul; and all that is within me,
> bless His holy name!
>
> Psalm 103:1 NKJV

What if today you came before the Lord for no other reason than to bless Him?

Too often, we make our prayers about ourselves. We come into His holy presence to receive. While it isn't wrong to ask Him for what we need, the greatest honor is to give. To set aside our agendas and simply love Him for who He is. To lavish Him with words of praise, thanks and dedication that overflow from a grateful heart.

How unfathomable that God, who created the heavens and the earth, is blessed by our frail, sometimes tainted love, but He is. And this magnificent One who continually pours out unspeakable provision for spirit, soul and body is worthy of our wholehearted devotion.

Your life becomes more enjoyable when you are not preoccupied with yourself. So how can you make today all about the Lord? With no list of requests, consider how to bless Him with your attention and affection, seeking nothing for yourself.

You bless the Lord when your only delight is to please Him and give Him the glory. Though your aim is to honor God, you can be assured that He will respond with far more than you are able to give. What a joy it is to bless the Lord!

REFLECT What would it look like to invest a day focused only on blessing the Lord with my attitude and actions?

PRAY Lord Jesus, I love You. It is my honor to worship You and to pour out tears of gratitude. Be blessed by my worship. Let the posture of my heart and the thoughts I think bring You glory. And may my passion to bless You, more than my desire to be blessed, become the motive behind all I do.

DECLARE I am a blessing to God.

ACT Ask the Holy Spirit to show you something you can do today—big or small—to bless God. Then do it.

12 | WILLING

Let my passion for life be restored, tasting joy in every breakthrough you bring to me. Hold me close to you with a willing spirit that obeys whatever you say.

Psalm 51:12 TPT

God is looking for your willing heart. But what can you do if you are struggling to surrender and obey?

Our Father knows every secret. He sees into the deepest caverns of our souls, where we often do not want to look. God is not surprised when we say we are willing to obey Him, yet our actions contradict our words. He does not condemn us. Instead, in love, He draws us close. It is from this place of love that we are inspired to do His will.

Jesus' pure, unconditional love gave Him the strength to lay down His life willingly. What an incredible example He gave us! The Lord knows that we sometimes battle to make costly sacrifices. He experienced this, even sweating great drops of blood, as He chose the Father's will (see Luke 22:42–44). When we understand the power of His love, we won't hesitate to ask Him to hold us close and *give* us a willing spirit. It is His joy to answer prayers like this.

God's love will soften your heart and change your mind. If you stay connected to His presence, willingness becomes effortless, and *yes* becomes your answer to whatever He asks.

REFLECT When do I struggle to have a willing spirit and therefore resist the Lord?

PRAY Father God, I want to do Your will, but sometimes I struggle and fight what is best for me. Come and hold me close. Refresh me. Give me a willing spirit as I bow my soul before You. Let Your love burn away double-mindedness and incinerate complacency. May I be Yours, completely.

DECLARE I have a willing spirit that obeys God.

ACT In an area that you have been fighting God, ask Him to give you a willing spirit.

13 | REMEMBER

"It shall be, when I bring a cloud over the earth, that the rainbow shall be seen in the cloud; and I will remember My covenant which is between Me and you and every living creature."

Genesis 9:14–15 NKJV

If it is important for God to remember His covenant promises, it is crucial that you do the same. Remembrance is key to a faith-filled, thankful heart.

Beneath the cloudy atmosphere of trials, there is a rainbow of promise. These promises may be painted on our hearts through God's Word by recalling prophetic encouragements, or by rehearsing the ways He has come through for us in the past. As we meditate on His faithfulness, it awakens hope. Remembering His goodness stirs joy and creates expectancy.

Forgetfulness often precedes unbelief. When we let the memories of His blessings slip away, we may be tempted to doubt. God ordained seasonal feasts for the nation of Israel to commemorate His provision and faithfulness. In His great wisdom, He calls us to reminisce and celebrate His blessings. Instead of focusing on negative memories, He invites us to saturate our minds with holy ones. It is difficult to feel discouraged and weary when declarations of thanksgiving and praise flood our hearts.

What are you remembering today? Put aside failures and disappointments except to learn from them, and be assured that the God who has been with you in the past walks with you today.

REFLECT Recall (and write down if you want) more than ten things God has done in your life.

PRAY Holy Spirit, awaken lost memories of Your goodness. As I set my attention on the many ways You've blessed me, lift my heaviness and fill my heart with joy. I will meditate on things that are lovely and of a good report. I will fill my heart with thankfulness, and let Your praise spill from my lips.

DECLARE I remember the goodness of the Lord.

ACT Share with someone the story of something significant God did for you in the past.

14 | STAND

Therefore take up the whole armor of God, that you may be able to withstand in the evil day, and having done all, to stand. Stand therefore.

Ephesians 6:13–14 NKJV

There is a time when you have done all you can, and all you can do is to stand firmly in the power of God.

Standing in your human strength can only take you so far. And fighting in your flesh for what can only be accomplished through the power of God will eventually lead to exhaustion.

But there is a higher way that makes no sense to the natural mind. It is the way of the Spirit, which stands upon a foundation of invisible truth. It is the solid path of prayer, which leads to long-awaited breakthrough.

In the moments when you have done all you know to do, God tells you to do one thing: stand in Him. Stand with your face toward heaven and your feet firmly planted in His truth. When you choose to live, move and exist in nothing other than Him, you will not be thrown off balance. All that you need is found in God.

What is the stand you have chosen to take? What stand is God asking you to take? Do all you know to do, but above all, rely on the Holy Spirit and His power to stand.

REFLECT In what area has God asked me to take a stand?

PRAY Steady Savior, You are the Faithful One. I lean on You, cry out to You and find victory in You. I don't have to do this on my own, fighting to keep my head above water. In the Holy Spirit I find an unending source of strength. Clothe me in Your light as I put on the armor that enables me to stand.

DECLARE I stand against evil by the power of the Holy Spirit.

ACT If you have become weary standing in faith or against evil, seek out another person today for encouragement and prayer.

15 | WORK

Whatever you do, work at it with all your heart, as working for the Lord, not for human masters.

Colossians 3:23 NIV

God created humans in His image and blessed them to be fruitful through work. All work is sacred when it is divinely inspired and empowered by the Holy Spirit. How do you perceive the work you do?

In a culture that prizes fame and fortune, we can chase work that draws us away from the Lord. We want the Lord to bless the work of our hands, but have we sought His wisdom and direction regarding our efforts?

Works of the flesh that are birthed by pride and contradict God's righteousness don't experience a great reward. When we humble ourselves and ask Him to lead, we taste His blessing on what we do because it is led by Him.

No matter what the work of our hands looks like, whether we feel it is significant or menial, God asks that we do it unto Him. We honor the Lord by diligently following His lead every day, seeking His guidance and grace. His blessing on all we do continues as we remain sensitive to the Holy Spirit.

You will find joy and satisfaction when you devote all your work—personal and professional—to the Lord. Wholehearted work is worship when we do it unto Him.

REFLECT How often do I find myself mindful of God's attention to and appreciation of my work?

PRAY Lord Jesus, I submit every dream, goal and endeavor to Your cleansing fire. Purify every desire and lead me by Your Spirit, so I'm never led by impure motives. You see everything I do, even the secret assignments that receive no recognition from man. May my work be done wholeheartedly, unto You, to bring You glory.

DECLARE God is my boss, and I work wholeheartedly for Him.

ACT Today, notice any time you find yourself looking for recognition from others. Then turn your attention to the Lord and hear His affirmation of your work.

16 | SURRENDER

Then Jesus said to His disciples, "If anyone desires to come after Me, let him deny himself, and take up his cross, and follow Me. For whoever desires to save his life will lose it, but whoever loses his life for My sake will find it."

Matthew 16:24–25 NKJV

Who doesn't want to experience the joys of a blessed life? But only those who are willing to surrender all will experience it.

It is easy to get excited about what Jesus has done for us and God's many amazing promises. We get less excited about Jesus' call to walk the path of holiness. We hold tightly to our opinions, desires and ways of living. We prioritize our comfort and happiness over the truth of God's Word and the leading of the Holy Spirit. Perhaps we forget that resurrection life only comes after death.

Jesus extended this invitation—to deny self, take up our cross and follow Him. Those who make these choices discover real life. When we surrender our will, fully trusting Him, peace becomes our new normal.

To see God's promises manifest, we must do our part. To hear His lovely voice, see His beautiful face and experience the glory of His presence, He must become our all. When we look for God wholeheartedly and unreservedly, we find Him.

Surrender will catapult you into a place of intimacy with the Lord because it removes barriers you have inadvertently placed there. You will find grace when you humble yourself and God's blessing when you relinquish your will to His.

REFLECT What area of my life continues to rule me because I have not surrendered it to Jesus?

PRAY Gracious Lord, I want unhindered, uninterrupted communion with You. I want to be Yours without reservation—every part of me consumed by Your purifying love. Give me the grace to surrender all. I'm willing, Lord. Reveal any area that has become an obstacle in our relationship, as I choose a lifestyle of absolute devotion and complete surrender to You.

DECLARE I surrender my life to Jesus.

ACT Do something today that demonstrates you are releasing control over an area of your life that God wants you to surrender to Him.

17 | WAIT

> Jesus instructed them, "Don't leave Jerusalem, but wait here until you receive the gift I told you about, the gift the Father has promised. For John baptized you in water, but in a few days from now you will be baptized in the Holy Spirit!"
>
> Acts 1:4–5 TPT

God wants to empower you to go, but the anointing of the Holy Spirit is imparted during times of waiting.

Before we can go and do, we must learn to stay and wait. Jesus said that He only did what He saw the Father doing (see John 5:19). This is the attitude of a patient and trusting heart—one that only moves when the Father says to move. When God stirs our hearts, we often want to forge ahead before pausing to discern His timing. Sometimes we prophetically know what God *will* do, but like Jesus, we must see what God is currently doing, so we can walk in agreement with Him.

For every assignment, we need a work of grace in our hearts. We need more than excitement. We need the tools of God's anointing, wisdom, compassion and discernment. We must know when to speak and what to say.

All you need for what the Lord wants you to accomplish is found in the place of waiting. This is where you mature and come face-to-face with your impatience. But as you cease from self-power and fully surrender your timetable to His, you become more like Jesus. Waiting is your place of empowerment.

REFLECT What am I waiting for in this season of my life?

PRAY Father of Glory, I want to know what is on Your heart and to see what You are doing. Enlighten the eyes of my understanding, so I will not step out of Your timing. I quiet my soul before You now and lean into Your presence and perspective. Here, in the wonder of Your love, I wait for Your direction and empowerment.

DECLARE I will wait and receive all God has for me.

ACT Wait longer than you normally would before making a final decision today. Take the extra time to receive insight and empowerment from the Holy Spirit.

18 | GO

"Go therefore and make disciples of all the nations, . . . and lo, I am with you always, even to the end of the age."

Matthew 28:19–20 NKJV

When Jesus gave His followers the commission to go, He never said to do it alone. He promised to be with them, and He will be with you, too.

The anointing to go is received in the patient attitude of waiting. Once we have the Father's instructions and are in unison with His timing, we have the partnership of His Spirit. When Jesus told us to go into all the world and shine our light, He also wanted us to be sensitive to the precise leading of the Holy Spirit. Every encounter with another person has a divine purpose, and God wants to show us how to uniquely release His heart to those we meet.

When you seek God's will, you will tap into His heart and be led by His Spirit. Your steps will be in sync with Him, and your words will be full of healing and life. Moment by moment, you will discern which situations need the light of His glory.

Going can be exciting, but it must be tempered by wisdom, obedience and the unction of the Holy Spirit. As His child, you are anointed to go, *as* He leads. You and the Holy Spirit working together are an unstoppable force.

REFLECT Where is God leading me to go today or in the near future?

PRAY Jesus, You are stirring my heart to partner with You in new ways. I know I cannot walk in the power of Your Spirit without being led by Your Spirit. Show me where to go. I am willing, and I am listening. As I follow Your command to go into the world today, may lives be impacted, and may You be glorified.

DECLARE God is with me as I go into the world.

ACT Point one person toward God in some way wherever you go today.

19 | FOCUS

> Looking to Jesus, the founder and perfecter of our faith, who for the joy that was set before him endured the cross, despising the shame, and is seated at the right hand of the throne of God.
>
> Hebrews 12:2 ESV

What fills your vision? What do you look at in times of trouble? Despite the turmoil you may be facing, you can choose to focus on the joy God has set before you.

Jesus suffered pain of body, soul and spirit in ways we cannot imagine. The sin and shame of the entire world was upon Him, yet by focusing on the promised blessing, He was able to endure until He accomplished His Father's will.

What was the joy set before Jesus? The salvation of the world and all those who would come to know Him. You were the joy set before Him. You are His reward.

To endure a "cross" you may be facing right now, set your focus on the One whose eyes have always been on you. When you keep the Lord as the center of your world, you will be able to brave the storms. His promises will anchor your soul. Gaze upon His face, and

His smile will calm your heart. Let your heart dwell on the One whose presence incinerates fear and sets faith ablaze.

Jesus was the founder of your faith, and He will perfect your faith. Push away anything that is crowding out a clear view of Him.

REFLECT Envision the extreme suffering and shame Jesus experienced so your sin could be forgiven and you could have an eternal relationship with Him.

PRAY Jesus, as I set my focus upon You, heaviness is melting away. You are so gracious and kind. Your love is extravagant and healing. You are looking back at me, and I feel the power of Your gaze igniting my faith. Distractions are fading away, and I can endure because I know You are sovereignly directing my life.

DECLARE The focus of my life is Jesus.

ACT Set two alarms today—one in the morning and one in the afternoon. When they go off, use the Reflect, Pray and Declare sections above to readjust your focus.

20 | ASK

"If you, imperfect as you are, know how to lovingly take care of your children and give them what's best, how much more ready is your heavenly Father to give wonderful gifts to those who ask him?"

Matthew 7:11 TPT

Every longing of your heart is important, not only to you, but also to your heavenly Father.

The petitions rising from your heart matter to Him. God-breathed desires are a gift the Lord has entrusted to you. He wants to pour life into each one as you lift it to Him in remembrance. Never be afraid to approach your Father to ask for what burns in your spirit. Every dream, promise and righteous longing is important. Though He often answers in ways you may not anticipate, His responses are always lifegiving and empowering.

Never feel that your desires are insignificant. God cares about everything that is in your heart. And when discouragement usurps your faith, let His presence reignite it. No matter how long you have waited, don't relent! God's timing is perfect, and while you have waited, He has been doing a work in your soul.

So, lift your voice and make your requests. Let the Lord resurrect every dead dream that you were never meant to forsake. Do not be silent! Ask in bold faith, remembering that the Lord loves to bless you. He is ready to give wonderful gifts to those who ask.

REFLECT How comfortable do I feel asking God for my needs *and* my desires?

PRAY Lord God, Your great love has ushered me before Your throne, so I may humbly present my requests. As I lean into you, create in me a clean heart so that all I ask is inspired by Your Holy Spirit. My confidence is in You alone. Thank You for caring about what is on my heart.

DECLARE I can ask because God lovingly cares for me, His child.

ACT Make an extravagant request of your heavenly Father.

21 | NEW

"I am doing something brand new, something unheard of. Even now it sprouts and grows and matures. Don't you perceive it? I will make a way in
the wilderness and open up flowing streams in the
desert."

Isaiah 43:19 TPT

You may feel dry, weary and uninspired, but hold on.
Something new is coming your way!

When life comes to a standstill, or things feel mun-
dane and boring, take time to rest and refuel. Seasons
like this are a prelude to something new. They lay the
groundwork for what God is about to do. During these
times, He is preparing you for what is coming. Though
you may experience frustration while waiting for the
next step, God is going to amaze and surprise you.

Don't be afraid to get excited. Behind the scenes,
the Lord is working on your behalf. He is about to release something unheard of in your life. Right in the
middle of your desert wilderness, where it seems you
have been left to fend for yourself, your Savior is about

to rush in like a flood! Like a fiery sunrise after the still of night, His blessings will color the horizon of your life.

If you are tired and have lost hope, allow the Spirit's fragrance of hope to revive your soul. Do you perceive God working in your life in a new way? If not, ask Him to show you what He is doing.

REFLECT What new thing am I anticipating from God, or what new thing do I see starting to sprout in my life in this season?

PRAY Heavenly Father, You stir my heart and awaken my hope. As I reach for You with expectation, speak and prepare me for all You have in store. You are paving a way right here in my wilderness and opening up refreshing streams in my desert. Thank You for doing something new in my life.

DECLARE God is doing something new in my life.

ACT Write down or tell a trusted friend the new thing you feel God is doing in your life, or what you want Him to do in your life.

22 | PROPHESY

> Again He said to me, "Prophesy to these bones,
> and say to them, 'O dry bones, . . . thus says the
> Lord GOD . . . "Surely I will cause breath to enter
> into you, and you shall live."'"
>
> Ezekiel 37:4–5 NKJV

God sees those who are dry and lifeless and is looking for those who will bravely and compassionately
become a mouthpiece of encouragement. As a child of
God, filled with His Spirit, you are a vessel for what He
wants to say to others.

Prophesying is simply hearing God's voice or per-
ceiving God's heart for someone and sharing it in a way
that person can receive. "Thus says the Lord," is not
needed. "Dry bones" are longing for Jesus, the Breath
of Life. You may or may not know the people He brings
across your path, but the Holy Spirit knows every secret of their lives and how to encourage them. Even
those who do not follow Jesus will recognize the heart
of the Father as it is released through you.

Pay attention to random thoughts and pictures that
rise within as you talk to people. Though they may not

make sense to you, as you stay aware of God's presence and release what He gives you, He will lead the conversation.

God has good plans for those around you, and He wants to convey them through you. His extravagant love will flow as you seek to edify and encourage others.

✺ **REFLECT** How comfortable do I feel encouraging others with what I hear from the Holy Spirit for them?

✺ **PRAY** Father God, I want to be a vessel of hope, edification and compassion. Holy Spirit, I avail myself to You today, and every day, for You to speak to me and through me. Give me Your heart for the people around me so that I may prophesy life into their dry bones.

✺ **DECLARE** I can hear God's voice and prophesy to others.

✺ **ACT** Ask the Holy Spirit to show you someone who needs encouragement today and prophesy to him or her.

23 | POWER

"You will receive power when the Holy Spirit comes
on you."

Acts 1:8 NIV

You are never powerless, even in your most devastated
state. You are powerful, but you can only do so much in
your own strength.

Stand in the assurance of this truth: The greatness
of the Almighty One lives inside of you. Remember who
you are in Him, and only because of Him. He is your
source of power, and His power is tireless, infinite and
eternal. It conquered death and now abides inside you
by the Holy Spirit.

The Holy Spirit also comes *upon* you to empower
words and actions according to His will. Natural might
and wisdom will only get you so far, but together with
God, you are unstoppable. Jesus instructed His followers to wait for the power of the Holy Spirit, not step
out and try to make things happen with their best prac-
tices. This precious and powerful Gift from God would
make their work fruitful and fulfilling.

Your power lies in your connection to God and
absolute dependence upon Him. He has already

conquered every obstacle. His ability replaces your inability. When His strength becomes yours, nothing is impossible! Do your part and exert wholehearted human effort, but do it with the power of the Spirit.

REFLECT What area of my life needs more of God's power?

PRAY Powerful God, I desire more than only what I can accomplish with my own power. Release in me and through me the power of the Holy Spirit. Empower me with Your loving presence. Keep me close to You in humble dependence. You make me brave and confident. Even when I feel weak, You are strong, and Your strength is unstoppable.

DECLARE The power of the Holy Spirit energizes everything I do.

ACT Focus prayerfully on one issue in your life (personal or professional) that has been stubborn to change. Ask the Holy Spirit for wisdom and to send His power for a breakthrough.

24 | DEAD

Likewise you also, reckon yourselves to be dead indeed to sin, but alive to God in Christ Jesus our Lord.

Romans 6:11 NKJV

Dead doesn't seem like a positive word, unless you consider that because of Christ, you are dead to your old way of doing things. You are no longer bound but free because dead people aren't restricted by sin, attitudes or anything else that inhibits God's glory.

When Jesus said to deny self, take up the cross and follow Him, it was an invitation to a lifestyle of freedom. The blessings of resurrection life only flow after death. Though it may seem difficult to die to fleshly ways, it only feels that way when our eyes are on what we think we are missing. If we set our eyes on all we gain and the inconceivable joys of knowing Jesus, we have no desire to sin intentionally. We become so caught up in the countless blessings of living daily with and for the Lord that we don't want anything to hurt that relationship.

Today, consider yourself dead, because in Christ you are. The old self is gone, and the new you in Christ is here (see 2 Corinthians 5:17). You are alive, created in the image of Christ and filled with the power of the Holy Spirit.

☀ **REFLECT** What is inhibiting my awareness of the Lord and His desires for today?

☀ **PRAY** Father of Life, I offer You every hindrance to our relationship. Shine on the areas of my life that don't reflect my desire to be entirely Yours. Deliver me from worldly thinking, opinions that don't reflect Yours and impure motives. Resurrect your glory in me, as I reckon myself dead to sin but alive in you.

☀ **DECLARE** I am dead to sin and alive to God in Christ Jesus.

☀ **ACT** When you are tempted or led astray from what God wants today, declare, "I am dead to [name the issue] and alive to God in Christ Jesus."

25 | SEEK

"And you will seek Me and find Me, when you search for Me with all your heart."

Jeremiah 29:13 NKJV

What are you searching for? If your heart is yearning to know the Lord in a deeper way, He will not disappoint. Even if you feel that your affections are scattered, but you continue to seek Him, He will graciously set everything else in order.

All you desire will fail in comparison when the Lord becomes your main passion. As you seek Him with *all* your heart, He proves repeatedly that He is all you need. Within God is the answer to everything. His love satisfies every craving of the soul.

Seeking the Lord is not expressed solely through prayer, Bible reading or attending a religious service; it is expressed by a posture of the soul, all day long. Even when the duties of life temporarily draw your thoughts away from the Lord, you are still moving toward Him when He is the object of your desire. The awareness of God and the humble position of continual seeking is evident as you gently return your attention to Jesus throughout the day.

As you go about the many activities of your day, ponder Scripture, whisper His name, invite the Spirit's presence, express gratitude and let worship rise. You will find Him.

REFLECT What treasures do you feel God is challenging you to seek out?

PRAY Jesus, You are the object of my desire. As I search for You, esteeming You more vital than my daily bread, I find You. One moment in Your presence drowns every distraction and brings into focus Your majesty. You are my treasure, my Friend, and with all my heart, I seek to know You more.

DECLARE My earnest desire is to seek the Lord.

ACT Ask two people what they perceive is the top priority you are seeking right now. Then agree in prayer with someone, asking the Holy Spirit's help to seek God with all your heart.

26 | CREATION

God's splendor is a tale that is told, written in the stars. Space itself speaks his story through the marvels of the heavens. His truth is on tour in the starry vault of the sky, showing his skill in creation's craftsmanship. Each day gushes out its message to the next, night with night whispering its knowledge to all. . . . Everywhere its message goes out.

Psalm 19:1–2, 4 TPT

Every day you are greeted by the beauty of God's creation. A carefully orchestrated symphony of love reaches out to remind you of His tender care and limitless power.

God has written a love story to you through creation—a daily reminder of life and hope. He wants you to be blessed by the diversity, magnificence and mystery of all He has given you. The Father wants you to slow down and take notice. He has filled the earth and sky with brilliant wonder for you to enjoy.

Every morning, the sun chases away the shadows. Each day, birds find food, and flowers awaken to refreshing dew. At night, the stars invite you to celebrate their Creator as you gaze upon their splendor. The signs of God's creative genius are all around if you will intentionally look for them. It is easy to remain hopeful and peaceful, and to believe you are loved, when you take the time to delight in the glory of creation.

Stand in awe of His magnificent handiwork, but remember—you are His most loved and cherished in all of creation.

REFLECT What is God's creation saying to me today?

PRAY Creator God, draw me by Your Spirit to notice the testaments of Your splendor around me. You truly are brilliant and creative. The colors You have painted in earth and sky, the refreshing waters and the fields that dance in invisible wind—everywhere I go, I am reminded of You.

DECLARE God uses His creation to draw me to Himself.

ACT Go outside and enjoy God's creation in some way today.

27 | FOLLOW

Jesus answered, "If I want him to remain alive until I return, what is that to you? You must follow me."

John 21:22 NIV

God has designed a path for you to follow. It is paved with precious stones and provisions for your journey. Though, at times, the way may feel treacherous and unclear, you can trust the Shepherd who leads you.

You are unique, and the direction the Lord is taking you is yours alone. It is specifically laid out according to the calling on your life. Don't become distracted by what others are doing. You have your own journey with the Lord. Hold tightly to His hand and listen to His instructions. Stay close to Jesus, your steps in sync with His, and His glory will illuminate your steps.

When your path veers in an unknown direction, contrary to what you expected, in the quiet of your heart, wait for the Holy Spirit to show you the way. Be careful not to fall into the trap of comparison or concern yourself with others' opinions. God will provide an inner peace greater than external disruptions.

Following is best done with your gaze set on the One you are following. He will most assuredly guide you on the paths right for your life, bringing honor to His name (see Psalm 23:3).

REFLECT What trick does the enemy use to keep me from following Jesus?

PRAY Father God, align my will with Yours. As I follow the path You have set before me, let Your grace keep me close, sensitive to every movement of Your Spirit. I may not always understand the direction You take me, but I trust You. You are for me, and You are the One I will follow.

DECLARE I follow Jesus, His teachings and example.

ACT Look for evidence that confirms you are actively following the guidance of the Holy Spirit today. Make changes based on what you see.

28 | FORGIVE

> But instead be kind and affectionate toward one
> another. Has God graciously forgiven you? Then
> graciously forgive one another in the depths of
> Christ's love.
>
> Ephesians 4:32 TPT

What causes an unpleasant stir in your emotions when
you think about it? God wants you to forgive and give
the person or situation to Him.

Almost everyone has experienced hurt, injustice and
mistreatment from others. Sometimes, it is crushing—
shaking us to the core and driving us to our knees. But
God, in His wisdom, asks us to go lower—to humble
ourselves and choose to forgive.

One of the most difficult choices we make is the decision to forgive, especially when we have the *right* to
be angry. We need justice. We want revenge. Our unre-
newed thinking wants to see those who hurt us suffer.
But mercy calls us to remember the cross. To stand before the One who gave everything so that we would be
forgiven. Though we don't deserve His mercy, He gives
it anyway. And now He calls us to do the same.

When Jesus suffered at the hands of His accusers, He chose to forgive and trust the Father for true justice. This humble act led to freedom and healing for the world. And as you follow His example, not seeking revenge, but forgiving as many times as it takes, you will also find freedom and healing for your heart.

REFLECT What people or situations inspire a rise of negative emotions when I think about them?

PRAY Holy Spirit, wash me with Your presence and cleanse my soul from bitterness and anger. Teach me to love. Pour into my heart the depths of Christ's love and His grace so I can forgive with sincerity. I release into Your hands my right for justice and trust You to make things right.

DECLARE God graciously forgave me; I willingly forgive others.

ACT For the first or fiftieth time, entrust into God's care someone you have had a hard time forgiving or something that continues to stir your emotions negatively.

29 | GLORIFY

"So, Father, bring glory to your name!" Then suddenly a booming voice was heard from the sky, "I have glorified my name! And I will glorify it through you again!"

John 12:28 TPT

You are a shining vessel of the Holy Spirit, who is the ultimate Source of every good thing. But who gets the glory when you experience this goodness and success?

It is easy to get sidetracked by success and be tempted to wear the praise of others as a crown, instead of laying it at the feet of Jesus. Our gifts, talents and anointings are given to us by God. They are facets of His brilliance that He has entrusted to us. He gives us everything we need to showcase His power, creativity, love and wisdom. What an incredible privilege to be living examples of our magnificent King.

We must remember that it is only by the impartation of His grace that we touch the people of the world and give them a glimpse of His glory. This awe-inspiring God leaves us wonderstruck. What else can we do but glorify the Lord for every good thing? To think that

He chooses to work through vessels of flesh is mind-boggling. May our attitudes, words and works point to the greatness of God.

God desires to glorify Himself through you today. Shine His light faithfully and point your success back to Him.

REFLECT What are a few creative, non-religious ways I can bring glory to God's name?

PRAY Marvelous God, You are magnificent and glorious in every way. Day after day You amaze me. I am in awe of You. Thank You for granting me the seemingly impossible privilege of partnering with You in the earth. Be glorified through me. May I never take the honor for myself.

DECLARE The Father glorifies His name through me.

ACT Publicly give credit to God today for something He has done that others could attribute to your own hard work.

30 | COME

"Are you weary, carrying a heavy burden? Come to me. I will refresh your life, for I am your oasis. Simply join your life with mine. Learn my ways and you'll discover that I'm gentle, humble, easy to please. You will find refreshment and rest in me."

Matthew 11:28–29 TPT

What do you expect from God when you come to Him? When Jesus says, "Come," He has refreshment, gentleness and rest waiting for you.

Your heavenly Father, who loves you unconditionally, is wooing you into the secret place of communion with the Spirit. Here, the glory of His presence falls like refreshing rain, washing away the dusty remains of worldly striving, busyness and distraction. No vacation can do what one moment in His arms can. No drug can imitate the bliss of being with Him. All you have to do is respond to His invitation by drawing close.

Come exactly as you are and learn how God handles burdens. You already have permission, and the angels of God are waiting to minister to you. In His presence waits revival and restoration. Jesus *is* the door into the most sacred place of all, and He is beckoning you to come. All that is required is a believing heart and a willingness to trust Him.

Today, still yourself beside His quiet waters and gaze upon His face. His glory will quench your thirst. Bring all weariness—every physical, mental and emotional strain of life—to Him, and you will find refreshment and rest.

REFLECT When I start to feel stress, where do I go first?

PRAY Welcoming Father, I accept Your invitation to come. Wrap me tightly in Your love so nothing steals my attention as I draw near. Teach me how to handle what comes my way today. Keep me revived and refreshed with the living water of Your Spirit. You are so gentle and humble. Who You are is wonderful.

DECLARE I find refreshment and rest every time I come to Jesus.

ACT Unload a heavy burden today through prayer and conversation with a trusted friend.

31 | PURSUIT

> Run as fast as you can from all the ambitions and
> lusts of youth; and chase after all that is pure. What-
> ever builds up your faith and deepens your love
> must become your holy pursuit.
>
> 2 Timothy 2:22 TPT

What is your primary pursuit? This Scripture instructs
you to pursue what builds up your faith and deepens
your love.

Chasing after what is pure includes running away
from what is unholy. If we desire to stand before the
Lord with pure hearts, we must be aware of where
our pursuits are leading us each day. There is nothing
wrong with setting goals, working hard and going after
our dreams, as long as these activities build up our faith
and deepen our love.

We should submit every pursuit to the Holy Spirit's
examination. Anything that pollutes our souls and sets us
up as lords over our lives will lead to an undesired end.

But pursuit does not happen by accident. Pursuit requires intention and action; otherwise life just happens
with the passing of time. When we actively "pursue

righteous living, faithfulness, love, and peace" (NLT), other areas align with His will for our lives.

Day-to-day busyness can keep you running fast, feeling productive but ultimately puzzled and empty. A primary role of the Holy Spirit in your life is to guide you into all truth (see John 16:13). Rest assured that anywhere the Holy Spirit leads is holy and worth pursuing.

REFLECT How do my primary pursuits build up my faith and deepen my love?

PRAY King Jesus, let nothing stand in the way of my pursuit of You and the Kingdom of God. I ask You to empower every holy pursuit by the Holy Spirit for right living, faithfulness, love and peace. Help me to remain in tune with Your Spirit. Refine every desire and guide every pursuit.

DECLARE I pursue what builds up my faith and deepens my love.

ACT Proactively take a step toward something you feel God is leading you to pursue.

32 | HUMILITY

God opposes the proud but gives grace to the humble.

James 4:6 ESV

If you feel the need for God's grace, His unmerited assistance, one sure way to receive it is to humble yourself.

God resists pride and those who embrace it. Proverbs 16:18 warns that pride goes before destruction, and Proverbs 6:17 lists a proud look as the first of seven things God detests. Why is God so opposed to pride and so in love with humility?

We are vessels of holiness and splendor, but with that blessing comes the responsibility to remember where that glory originated. We are only dust, a passing wind. We are entirely dependent upon God. Every success, each moment of favor and recognition, even our ability to breathe comes from Him. Though we are to carry ourselves as vessels of royalty, this can only be accomplished through humility—knowing who has bestowed this blessing upon us.

The grace of God flows freely when we walk humbly with the Lord and seek to glorify Him. When we make ourselves of no reputation, regardless of our positions in worldly systems, we enjoy the highest honor— exalting God alone and bringing glory to His name.

The Holy Spirit wants to assist you today as you choose deliberately to walk in humility.

REFLECT When have I felt God resisting me, and when have I felt His grace?

PRAY Humble Savior, I want to honor You in all I say and do. Cleanse me of selfishness and pride. Forgive me for pointing to myself instead of seeking to glorify You for Your marvelous works. It is only by grace that I stand, and only because of the Holy Spirit that I will have crowns to lay at Your feet.

DECLARE I walk in humility and receive God's grace.

ACT In an area where you have expressed pride in the past, demonstrate humility today.

33 | DWELL

He who dwells in the secret place of the Most High shall abide under the shadow of the Almighty.

Psalm 91:1 NKJV

God invites you to retain—not just access on occasion—a secret space in your heart for His presence. Under His shadow you will find peace and rest.

To dwell with God is to share every moment with Him—to enjoy sacred friendship and to include Him in everything you do. Throughout the day, you fix your thoughts and desires on Him, continually returning your attention to the One who loves you. When knowing Him, loving Him and living for Him is your desire, it isn't an inconvenience to live this way. You are effortlessly drawn by the love and fellowship of the Holy Spirit.

Despite any chaos happening *around* you, you can determine what happens *within* you by choosing where your soul dwells. Will you abide in the place of His presence uniquely set apart for you, or will you visit it occasionally, instead deciding to dwell in stress or unrest?

Do not be tempted to dwell anywhere except under the shadow of Almighty God. He will be your place of safety and strength—physical, mental, emotional and spiritual. Regardless of your responsibilities today, dwelling—remaining and abiding—in the secret place is possible.

REFLECT Where do I feel safest, and where do I like to rest?

PRAY Almighty God, stir the fragrance of Your presence in my life so I'm continually aware of how close You are. I want to live in Your eternal, abiding glory. Regardless of where I go and what I do, I want to dwell with You and remain conscious of the blessing of our friendship.

DECLARE I dwell with God and find permanent shelter under His shadow.

ACT Create a detailed picture in your mind of what it is like to dwell under the shadow of the Almighty. When you think of Psalm 91, visualize your secret place with God.

34 | STOP

> Remind everyone about these things, and command them in God's presence to stop fighting over words. Such arguments are useless, and they can ruin those who hear them.
>
> 2 Timothy 2:14 NLT

The words you speak carry the power of life and death (see Proverbs 18:21). They are either fueled by God's heart or represent the enemy's desire for destruction.

Arguing does not showcase the wisdom and heart of God, even if your stance seems righteous. Very little good comes from pushing your viewpoint upon people whose hearts are closed to hearing it. To force your opinion, even if you feel it matches God's, is to fight for your agenda. Quarrels and fights are mostly self-serving, and do not represent God's heart properly.

God knows some personalities are more passionate, courageous and confrontational, but when you genuinely speak the mind of Christ with the love of Christ, it is more likely that hearts will be softened, convicted and changed. Ephesians 4:29 says to let no corrupt talk come from your mouth, but only what builds up others.

The Holy Spirit wants to use your words to give grace to those who hear.

Stop getting drawn into meaningless arguments, and avoid talk that only serves to make you feel superior to others. Seek out what the Holy Spirit wants to say. He will not only give you words, but He will also help you say them.

☀ **REFLECT** What kind of words do I most want to stop coming from my mouth?

☀ **PRAY** Father God, forgive me for opening my mouth and letting useless, hurtful and selfish words spill out. Give me Your tender heart in every conversation, especially the difficult ones when I don't agree with someone. Holy Spirit, help me demonstrate the character of Christ with the words of my mouth. May they be pleasing to You and give grace to those who hear.

☀ **DECLARE** I will stop useless communication and speak words of grace.

☀ **ACT** Fill your mouth with the opposite of the type of words that you want to stop. For example, if you want to stop criticizing others, intentionally compliment someone today.

35 | OBEDIENCE

> "But this is what I commanded them, saying, 'Obey My voice, and I will be your God, and you shall be My people. And walk in all the ways that I have commanded you, that it may be well with you.'"
>
> Jeremiah 7:23 NKJV

Obedience is a primary way to demonstrate your trust in God and commitment to Him. It isn't always easy, but it is always worth it.

There is a cost to walking closely with the Lord; it is the price of obedience. Jesus obeyed to the point of death, and we are called to do the same—to sacrifice earthly desires on an altar of holy devotion. We commit ourselves to Him, knowing that whatever He requires is for our good and produces a deeper connection to Him. Yes, we feel the sting of doing the difficult things God asks, but He has promised that as we walk in His ways, it will be well with us.

Obeying the Lord, even when we don't see the full picture and step out on nothing but faith, sets us apart as God's people. It is the evidence of a heart completely sold out to God. Here, in the place of uncompromising commitment, we are transformed into His likeness and open the door for the Holy Spirit to do what only He can do.

When you hear God speak, quickly respond. Obedience motivated by love and gratitude will draw you closer to Jesus.

REFLECT What is something God has asked me to do that I have yet to obey Him in completely?

PRAY Lord Jesus, I desire to obey You in every way. Forgive me for not obeying You after hearing You speak to my heart. Give me a clean heart and a willing spirit to respond quickly and to do whatever You say with joy. Holy Spirit, change my attitude where necessary, and pour out Your grace as I walk the path of obedience today.

DECLARE Obedience keeps me walking on God's path for my life.

ACT Follow through with complete obedience in something God has asked you to do.

36 | WITH

May the grace of the Lord Jesus Christ, and the love of God, and the fellowship of the Holy Spirit be with you all.

2 Corinthians 13:14 NIV

You are not alone, and you will never be alone. The triune God—Father, Son and Spirit—is always with you.

This blessing from the apostle Paul weaves together three very powerful elements into a promise for us today: The grace of Jesus, the love of God the Father and the fellowship with the Holy Spirit will be with us. Jesus' grace keeps us walking by faith and following Him as Lord; the Father's love provides the lens through which we interpret life; and the active presence of the Holy Spirit comforts, counsels and encourages.

A uniqueness of the God of the Bible, versus the gods of other religions, is that He wants to be with His people. One Hebrew name for God is *Immanuel,* which means "God is with us." John 3:16 says that God so loved the world He sent His Son, Jesus, so we would not have to remain separated from God and perish because of our sin. Instead, we can have eternal life . . . with Him.

Before Jesus ascended to heaven, He promised, "Be sure of this: I am with you always, even to the end of the age" (Matthew 28:20 NLT). You can *be sure* that God is with you today.

REFLECT How certain am I of God's presence with me? How does that perception affect my decisions?

PRAY Triune God, what a privilege it is to know You personally. With gratitude I embrace the grace of my Lord and Savior, Jesus Christ. Thank You for revealing the Father's love to me and for the daily fellowship I have with the Holy Spirit. Help me perceive more strongly Your presence with me. I want to be confident of Your nearness.

DECLARE God's grace, love and presence are always with me.

ACT Picture Jesus next to you today, wherever you are, whatever you are doing. Talk to Him like you would talk to a person sitting next to you and enjoy the presence of His Spirit with you.

37 | BOAST

"But let the one who boasts boast about this: that
they have the understanding to know me, that I
am the Lord, who exercises kindness, justice and
righteousness on earth, for in these I delight," declares the Lord.

Jeremiah 9:24 NIV

What do you boast about? If you are going to boast
about anything, boast that you know God and understand that He is the Lord.

God, who is gracious and kind, invites us into the
greatest blessing of all—to know Him. He doesn't stand
far off, as a Creator disconnected from His creation.
He comes right up to us, pulls us close, and with excitement, offers friendship, partnership and unity. God sets
a table of fellowship and makes Himself known to those
whose hearts are after His. What an extraordinary gift!

Though we don't deserve it, we can know the Ruler
of the Universe. We can dive into the expanse of God's
love and call Him Father, Savior and Friend. He wants to
reveal the secrets of His heart to us. This is something
we can boast about and rejoice in! This kind of boasting

is not prideful because it has nothing to do with us. All praise highlights His amazing grace and lovingkindness.

When you boast about the Lord, you are directing the glory to Him. Today, make a pure and holy declaration of who God is, because, by His grace, you know Him.

REFLECT What has God done in my life that I can boast about?

PRAY Almighty God, I am in awe that You have invited me to understand You. Holy Spirit, open the eyes of my understanding to grow in the knowledge of God. I am seeking You—not just for what You give but for who You are. My heart is overflowing with gratefulness, and I'm boasting in You!

DECLARE My boast is in a kind, just, righteous Lord.

ACT Boast about God—who He is or what He has done—to someone today.

38 | EMPTY

> [Jesus] emptied himself of his outward glory by
> reducing himself to the form of a lowly servant.
> He became human!
>
> Philippians 2:7 TPT

Empty may seem like a negative word, but it is what allowed Jesus to fulfill His calling, relate to humanity and bring salvation to the world.

Before being born as a human baby on this earth, Jesus had eternally existed as the Word, who "gave life to everything that was created" and "brought light to everyone" (John 1:4–5 NLT). When Jesus gave up His divine privileges as God and became human, He gave us a model to follow. Imagine the eternal Word emptying Himself of His outward glory and confining Himself to a human body!

But this act of true humility is what helped us know the infinite, all-powerful Creator we have not seen. Jesus showed us in person what the Father is like through His character, attitude, words and daily choices. He demonstrated how to partner with the Spirit to work wonders. And He showed how to surrender fully, even when He could have called thousands of angels to save Him from death.

Your position in life may have afforded you some privileges—wealth, notoriety, wisdom, talents and connections. Today, follow Jesus' example so you can better relate to those around you and show them what God is like.

☀ **REFLECT** How can I become more "human" so that others can relate better to me, opening a door to serve them and show them what God is like?

☀ **PRAY** All-Sufficient One, I bow before You and empty myself of all You have given to me. I do this so others will see Your glory and come to know You, too. Holy Spirit, give me the same attitude Jesus had so I can humble myself and be approachable, serving others with joy and tender love.

☀ **DECLARE** I empty myself to be more like Jesus.

☀ **ACT** Relate to another person today in a way that he or she understands best.

39 | FLEE

> She caught [Joseph] by his garment, saying, "Lie with me." But he left his garment in her hand, and fled and ran outside.
>
> Genesis 39:12 NKJV

There is a time to fight, and a time to flee. When enticed by his boss's wife, Joseph's response is one to emulate—remove yourself from the temptation as quickly as possible.

The enemy doesn't play fair. He knows what causes us to stumble. He preys on our emotional, physical and mental weaknesses, doing everything he can to trick us into staying in a fight Jesus has already won. Whether we are being lured into arguments or offense, enticed by sexual sin, or tempted to doubt God's love, fleeing into the safety of God's embrace is the way to break free.

Do not waste a moment analyzing the bait dangling in front of you. Refuse to entangle yourself with lesser things. You are destined for greatness, so trust in God's ability to keep you from stumbling. The Holy Spirit will help you choose the path that leads *away* from evil and *toward* God's goodness.

Joseph did not flee because he was a coward; he fled because he cared deeply about his relationship with God and did not want to engage with evil. Today, be alert and have the courage to walk away from whatever is not in God's best interest for you.

REFLECT What has ensnared me in the past that I need to be prepared to flee in the future?

PRAY Holy Spirit, help me to discern the temptations and traps the enemy sets for me. Give me courage and strength to flee quickly from each one. I desire to run the race You have set before me successfully and not become entangled in sin. Your grace is sufficient for me as I choose the path of integrity, purity and faith.

DECLARE I will flee from evil and run toward what is good.

ACT Recognize when the enemy is baiting you to remain when you are supposed to flee. Exit the situation and enter God's presence.

40 | WISDOM

The wisdom that is from above is first pure, then peaceable, gentle, willing to yield, full of mercy and good fruits, without partiality and without hypocrisy.

James 3:17 NKJV

Human wisdom is helpful, but wisdom from above exceeds every expectation of what you can come up with on your own.

James 1:5 (NLT) declares, "If you need wisdom, ask our generous God, and he will give it to you." Your heavenly Father loves you and hasn't left you to figure out things on your own. He is with you, ready to step into the situations that have you stumped. Every conversation, each endeavor and all your daily decisions go much more smoothly when you let Him guide you with His wisdom.

God *is* perfect wisdom. The fruit of the wisdom God gives aligns with His character. Everything He does, is and ever will do is intentional, pure, peaceable, gentle, humble, full of mercy and without hypocrisy. As His children and representatives on earth, we are meant to emulate this kind of wisdom.

Turn your attention to the Lord and wait for His wisdom. Do not wrestle, analyze or strive for a solution that can only be found in a posture of absolute dependence upon God. He is eager to hear you ask for help, and He will give you wisdom from above today.

REFLECT In what area of my life do I need God's wisdom today?

PRAY Lord Jesus, I do not want to face today without You, and I'm so glad that I don't have to! Lead me by Your Spirit and instruct me. I lay my plans, ideas and earthly understanding at Your feet, and receive wisdom from above, which is pure, gentle and peaceable. Help me to represent You well as I share what You have given to me with others.

DECLARE God generously gives me wisdom when I ask.

ACT Ask God for His wisdom today about a specific situation, place your faith in God alone for the result, and act upon it.

41 | FATHER

For you did not receive the spirit of bondage again to fear, but you received the Spirit of adoption by whom we cry out, "Abba, Father."

Romans 8:15 NKJV

Before you took your first breath, you were known and loved by God the Father in heaven. You were chosen, wanted and wonderfully created in His heart, and through Jesus He has made every provision for you to know Him as Father.

If you have received Jesus, you are no longer a spiritual orphan. You have been joyfully adopted into God's family. All of heaven stands in awe of the eternal, life-giving relationship granted to you, God's child. Your heavenly Father wants to be with you forever. He will never abandon you. Even on your worst day, He is cheering you on and declaring your worth. Do you believe that?

You may need to renew your mind about what you feel God the Father is like. Personal tragedies and world calamities can paint the Father as abusive or absent. Or maybe an earthly parent, caregiver or spiritual leader has let you down, and you have blamed Father God.

God's care, however, is unmatched. He knows when to hold you close and when to let you run.

As a child of God, you are led by the Spirit of God. Today, invite the Spirit to lead you into a more accurate revelation of your heavenly Father and His outrageous love for you.

REFLECT How has the relationship with my earthly father or a spiritual leader affected my perception of the heavenly Father?

PRAY Heavenly Father, Your love is healing, constant and true. I never have to wonder how You feel about me because You prove Your love every day. I sense Your nearness. Draw me closer. How blessed I am to be Your child and to know that I am precious in Your eyes. Help me to know You more.

DECLARE My heavenly Father loves me and has adopted me into His family.

ACT Do something kind for a child today and tell him or her, "God loves you." Then consider that your gesture was just a small token of the boundless love the Father has for you.

42 | FEAST

> "I will feed you with my spiritual bread. You will feast and be satisfied with me, feeding on my revelation-truth like honey dripping from the cliffs of the high place."
>
> Psalm 81:16 TPT

Every day, you can choose to feast on spiritually nutritious bread from heaven or settle for spiritual junk food. Which will you choose?

Step into the banqueting hall of our extravagant God. He has set a feast before you—a medley of truths to feed your soul. The feast is a celebration of His goodness and mercy. Here in God's presence is everything you could ever want. Revelations drip like honey.

Eating spiritual bread may sound mysterious, but you were created to partake of the Bread of Life. To feast on God's love is to taste and see that He is good (see Psalm 34:8). It is as simple and glorious as filling yourself with Him every day and "eating" the truth He offers. Feasting is basking in His lifegiving and sustaining love, while recognizing the blessing of His presence. When God becomes your holy preoccupation, the cravings for temporary distractions fade. Your eyes open to fresh insight, understanding and revelation. Soon, nothing else satisfies, and He becomes your everything.

When God prepares a feast for you, do not take just a little bite. Consume all God lays before you. Go all in and be completely satisfied.

REFLECT What is the feast God is preparing for me?

PRAY Giver of All Good Things, the way You care for me is astounding. Every part of me reaches to partake of the holy and extravagant feast You set before me. Nothing satisfies me like You do. All that You offer overwhelms me in the best possible way. I am completely satisfied when I eat from Your hand.

DECLARE I will feast and be satisfied with the Lord.

ACT Go all in and completely feast on something God has given to you.

43 | KNOWN

Lord, you know everything there is to know about me. You perceive every movement of my heart and soul, and you understand my every thought before it even enters my mind.

Psalm 139:1–2 TPT

No one knows you as the Lord does. Every thought, motive and desire has His attention.

He takes time to number each hair and is faithful to grant every breath. Jesus sees what others miss because He examines us to the depths of spirit and soul—not to point out all that is bad, but to draw out the goodness of His likeness in us. He knows us better than we know ourselves. Nothing about us is overlooked or unknown, and everything is covered by mercy—every sin, shortcoming and failure.

Only someone absolutely smitten with you would take the time to know you so well. And, with the same intensity and passion that God acquaints Himself with you, He draws you close so that you may know Him. What a joy to be known by the King of all!

While the Lord already knows everything there is to know about you, He still loves to hear you share what is on your heart. Talk to God today and listen as He speaks back to you. If He is quiet, remain beside Him and become comfortable in the silence. It is there that you will discover the secrets of His heart.

REFLECT What do I think the Lord enjoys the most about me?

PRAY Omniscient God, I am in awe that You love me the way You do. You know what is going on in my heart and mind, and You understand me completely. It is good to be thoroughly known and fully loved by You. Reveal more of Yourself to me, Lord, and help me to know myself better, too.

DECLARE Everything about me is known by God, and He still loves me.

ACT Tell the Lord something today that you have kept only to yourself.

44 | FIRE

"[Jesus] will baptize you with the Holy Spirit and fire."

Luke 3:16 ESV

Fire has many functions. God graciously provides fire in your life for purification and power.

God, in His great mercy, responds to our cries for purity. God's heart is moved when we stand before Him, longing to have no barriers between us. When we open ourselves to His cleansing fire, unafraid of the consuming flames, it results in inexplicable freedom. God will not ignore us, especially when we feel dry and weary. Nothing escapes the fires of His passion when a soul desires it.

Lay the pieces of your life before Him, in absolute trust. Wait for His breath to ignite every flickering ember. Hold nothing back from the One who is trustworthy, holy and pure. Surrender every concern, doubt and fear, and ask the Lord to cleanse every area of your life until your entire being blazes with unquenchable desire to be unreservedly His.

This fire will change you—alter you at the very core. Love will transform your heart and ignite holy passion

until everything that stood in the way turns to ash.
God's fire will also empower you to be a living witness
for Christ, walking in the likeness of His character and
miraculous works.

REFLECT What do I want the fire of the Holy Spirit to
do in my life?

PRAY Holy Spirit, let Your fire fall upon my heart.
Transform me—spirit, soul and body—with Your
cleansing glory. May the heart embers that barely flicker
turn into a blazing fire that burns fervently for You. Fire
of God, by Your mercy and grace, let my life ignite an
unrelenting hunger in others to know You.

DECLARE The fire of the Holy Spirit purifies and em-
powers me.

ACT Observe where you see the Holy Spirit working
to purify or empower you. Do something today to cooperate with His work in this area.

45 | FAITHFUL

Your faithfulness extends to every generation, as
enduring as the earth you created.

Psalm 119:90 NLT

God's faithfulness is behind countless miracles in your
life. Remembering His goodness inspires gratitude and
produces breakthrough into new miracles.

The sun, moon and stars unceasingly remind us that
the Creator can be trusted. Each breath is proof that
God is with you. Despite the trials we endure, God is
with us, ready to show how He turns things around for
our good.

When shadows of doubt obscure your vision, it is
important to reflect on what He has done in the past.
Let memories of previous victories flood your thinking.
Speak about them, write them down and let thankfulness rise. As you do, faith throws open the door for another victory! This is the attitude that attracts blessing
and dispels discouragement. Faith pleases God because
it believes in His extraordinary love and kindness.

If fear or hardship has talked you out of the radi-
cal faith you once had, shake it off. Begin to praise the

Lord for the many times He has come through for you. Though you may not feel like it, sing, dance and shout this truth—God is good! He is faithful!

God loves you, and He is turning things around.

REFLECT What am I trusting God for right now?

PRAY Lord God, You have been faithful to me in the past, and Your faithfulness will continue every day of my life. Remind me of our history together, of how You have been steadfast in Your love and care for me. I desire to step into every one of Your promises by faith. You love me, and You prove it every single day.

DECLARE God is always faithful.

ACT Recall the many times you have seen God's faithfulness. Thank Him out loud for each.

46 | FRIEND

"Now you are my friends, since I have told you everything the Father told me."

John 15:15 NLT

Friendship with God is a blessing that cannot be compared to any other relationship. This gift will touch every part of your life.

Friendship with God affects your conversations and decisions throughout your day. But most of all, it gives substance to your faith. When you live each day in continual communication with the Holy Spirit, valuing this tremendous gift, it gives you courage. Being a friend of God means that you always have Someone to confide in, laugh with and spend time with. It means you have Someone who always believes in you and knows exactly how to cheer you up.

But like all good friendships, you must not focus on yourself. This is a pure friendship that gives and receives—caring as deeply about the Lord's desires as He cares about yours.

Tend to your friendship with God today. Spend time getting to know Him and listening to what is on His heart. Honor the Holy Spirit by walking and talking with Him throughout the day, and discover how fun and rewarding it is to relate to your Creator as a friend.

REFLECT What do I enjoy doing with friends? Would I do the same with God?

PRAY Jesus, I'm so blessed to be Your friend! Thank You for always having my back and for caring about aspects of my life that only a close friend would care about. I want to know what's on Your heart and to recognize Your voice among a thousand other voices. Help me to cherish our friendship and never take it for granted.

DECLARE I am a friend of God.

ACT Do something with God today that you would normally do with a close friend.

47 | WORSHIP

"You must worship the LORD your God and serve
only him."

Luke 4:8 NLT

God created you to worship. Directing your attention
and devotion to God in worship releases your heart and
refreshes your soul.

God is worthy of your worship, regardless of how
your day is going. If you are disappointed, turn your
heart to the Lord and release your frustration. If blessings abound and more are on the way, pour out songs
of gratitude. Look to Jesus and remember the enormity
of His love.

As worship surges through your being, the Holy
Spirit destroys fear and knocks down walls of opposition. Worship helps you refocus so you can see from
God's perspective. Worship reminds you of His om-
nipotence and leaves you awestruck.

When honest words of surrender and adoration to
Jesus rise from your heart, and you look past the good
and bad around you to focus only on Jesus, you are
worshiping in spirit and truth. When you are intent on

blessing Him, instead of being blessed, you discover the purity of worship and are drawn into a place of holy bliss. God always gives back more than we can give.

Do you sense the Holy Spirit drawing you into His presence? God is worthy of your time and attention in worship today.

REFLECT When have I experienced worship that has left me a different person because of my encounter with God?

PRAY Precious Jesus, the depths of Your glory are calling to the depths of my being. It is my joy to respond in worship. I honor You and desire to lavish upon You unrestrained devotion. I come before You today, simply to bless You. May every word be sincere as I lift my worship to You. You are worthy of my time and attention.

DECLARE I give Jesus all my worship.

ACT Set aside time today to worship God—with song, action or silent admiration.

48 | THANKFUL

Be thankful in all circumstances, for this is God's will for you who belong to Christ Jesus.

1 Thessalonians 5:18 NLT

Your day will be full of blessings. But are you aware of this, or do you only notice when something goes wrong?

It's sad to say that we often don't pay attention to our blessings until they're gone or temporarily removed. We may not be thankful for our health until we feel sick. We may take relationships, jobs or favor for granted until those things get shaken. We overlook significant blessings because we're busy asking for something else. But what if we focused our energy on being grateful for what we have and trusted God with everything we're waiting for?

Being grateful changes your disposition. It's hard to be anxious, stressed or depressed when thinking about the joys in life. There is a healing and life-altering shift when you intentionally look for things that warm your heart or make you happy.

Whether it's something insignificant, like a stranger's smile or a gentle breeze, or something necessary, like the roof over your head, every time you notice these gifts from God, thank Him. With intentionality, make it a habit to look for the good in your life. There's always something to be thankful for.

☀ **REFLECT** How would my emotions be impacted if I spent the day being thankful?

☀ **PRAY** Father God, forgive me when I've taken any of Your blessings for granted. I am wonderfully blessed, more than I deserve. Complaining about what's wrong isn't going to bring breakthrough; instead, I'm going to praise You and focus on the joys You've set before me. Holy Spirit, help me recognize Your blessings and become a thankful person.

☀ **DECLARE** I am thankful in every situation I face.

☀ **ACT** Be extravagantly thankful today—all day, to everyone, for everything.

49 | DELIGHT

> Take delight in the LORD, and he will give you the desires of your heart.
>
> Psalm 37:4 NIV

What makes your heart rejoice? Many things compete for your attention, but when you delight in the Lord, He gives you the desires He has placed in your heart.

The superficial things that fight for priority aren't worthy of being compared to the One whose glory fills our beings. When we ponder His goodness, lavish Him with praise, choose His will over our own or love others when we would rather be dismissive, we are making God our delight.

When enjoying the Lord and living for Him becomes our focus, everything else takes second place. Yes, we still have needs and other desires, but when love for Him consumes us, prayer lists don't seem as important. Even times of intercession feel effortless and assured because we're flowing in agreement with His Spirit.

The affections of your heart and mind set the tone, not only for the day but for your entire life. Delighting in the Lord may not immediately change the trials you face, but it causes faith to frame your perspective and releases God's wisdom into your life. This posture of devotion also releases peace and joy into every situation.

While you are busy delighting in Jesus and discovering His desires, He will surprise you by taking care of things that once held your attention.

REFLECT When did God give me a desire of my heart? How was it connected to my delight in Him?

PRAY Father of Lights, You make my soul sing! Nothing compares to You. No one holds my heart so carefully and makes me feel so alive. When I delight in You, You faithfully bring my desires to life. I enjoy You and am enriched when I invest time in Your presence. You are my joy and great reward, and I delight in You.

DECLARE My delight is in the Lord.

ACT Express your delight in the Lord in a tangible way today.

50 | HONOR

Love one another with brotherly affection. Outdo one another in showing honor.

Romans 12:10 ESV

In a world full of cultural, political, social and religious diversity, how do you honor those you disagree with? And how can you best represent Jesus in every conversation?

A lifestyle of honoring the Lord includes honoring others. That doesn't mean that you refrain from hard conversations or let others walk over you to avoid conflict. Honest communication must be done with the knowledge that the person you're speaking to is loved and cherished by God. When His love for others fills your heart, it will be easily heard in the tone of voice and the look in your eyes.

Honoring others is much easier when you have spent time in the presence of God. When you carry His heart, you want to treat those He loves with dignity and respect. Jesus ate with sinners and offered the lost a seat at His table. Honoring others makes you stand out in a crowd. People may not agree with you, but if you walk in love, they will be less likely to feel judged or disrespected.

In every conversation, keep mercy before you; it will keep you humble and able to honor people, even if you believe they are wrong and you are right.

REFLECT What are different ways I can show honor to those who deserve it *and* to those who do not?

PRAY Honorable Father, thank You for reminding me that You love and highly value people because they are created in Your image. Help me extend mercy and bestow honor to others, even if I don't agree with them. Teach me to love unconditionally with healthy boundaries in place. May every word I speak reflect Your stance of humility and honor.

DECLARE I love others and show honor consistently.

ACT Outdo yourself and show honor to two people today: one who really deserves it, and one whom you feel does not.

51 | SPLENDOR

I will meditate on your majestic, glorious splendor
and your wonderful miracles.

Psalm 145:5 NLT

What captivates you? Today the Lord is drawing you to
meditate on His majestic, glorious splendor.

Those whose souls yearn to see the glory of the
Lord live differently. We have tasted and seen that He
is good, and we are eternally changed. One glimpse of
God's splendor has left us joyously longing for more.
Every moment holds an opportunity to behold Him.
Whether alone in His presence or standing before
majestic mountains, we find God's glory etched into all
we see.

The One who throws the sky open like a curtain
wants us to enjoy His beauty, and we are intent on
discovering it everywhere we go. From the heights of
heavenly places, where He has invited us to sit, we see
every situation from God's perspective. All things can
be made beautiful. All situations, people and places
were created to display His glory. This is His desire—to
fill the world with reflections of His brilliance.

So today, look for His smile on a stranger's face. Don't take the sunrise for granted. Sit beneath the stars. Enjoy the clouds with childlike imagination. Pay attention to the joys of the season. God's splendor is all around you.

REFLECT Where have I been or what have I seen that represents for me the splendor of God?

PRAY Father of Glory, I'm awestruck by the hues of Your splendor around me. Here, in the quiet of my heart, I see and feel You. Everywhere I go, glimpses of glory surprise me. You paint the sky just for me. You are magnificent, reaching for me with beauty and extravagance that awakens my heart.

DECLARE God's glorious splendor and wonderful miracles captivate my attention.

ACT Look at pictures that demonstrate God's majestic, glorious splendor.

52 | COURAGE

"Be strong and courageous. Do not be afraid or ter-
rified because of them, for the LORD your God goes
with you; he will never leave you nor forsake you."

Deuteronomy 31:6 NIV

What has God asked you to do? If desires are burning
in your heart, but fear is blocking your path, look to
Him. Don't talk yourself out of what God wants to do
through you.

Courage comes when you know the Spirit of God
who stands with you. The more you know the Lord, and
the greater your acceptance of His love for you, the
easier it is to step out in confidence. When you spend
time with Him, not only to discuss what's on your mind
but to hear what's on His, the Holy Spirit ignites a fire
of desire that compels you to do what you never dared
to do before.

When you're united with the Lord, wholly submit-
ted to Him, it's hard to tell the difference between your
desires and His. You are one with Him, and when you
know God's Spirit is directing you, fear no longer holds
you back. Though your mind may try to convince you

that faith is crazy, when you have His word, you boldly take the risk, even if it's done with apprehension.

Today, step out! Be courageous. The Lord is on your side, and He goes with you. Stay close to Him because He makes you brave.

※ **REFLECT** Where in my life do I need the most courage?

※ **PRAY** Bold Savior, You are empowering me today. Give me the courage to do what You have set before me. Holy Spirit, counsel me, give me wisdom and make a way where there seems to be no way so that I can do Your will. By Your grace and with Your strength, fear will not hold me back.

※ **DECLARE** The Holy Spirit gives me strength and courage.

※ **ACT** Step out courageously in some way today.

53 | GENEROUS

"For God so loved the world that He gave His only begotten Son, that whoever believes in Him should not perish but have everlasting life."

John 3:16 NKJV

The Father was never more generous than when He chose to give His Son, Jesus, who in turn gave His life for the world's salvation. He invites you to follow this example.

Our generous, over-the-top Father is extravagant in every way. Not only has He given us the gift of salvation, but every day He makes Himself available to us. Every moment He lavishes us with treasures of life and hope that are found in Him. He never stops giving to us—freely, intentionally, generously. The tremendous outpourings of affection never stop, and they are not contingent upon anything we do. He loves, simply because it's His nature.

You were created in His image, and you have the privilege of following in His footsteps. Take the cue and learn from Him, looking for ways to bless others. Receiving is fun, but giving makes you more like your heavenly Father. When you consider others, remembering how much God cherishes them, you become an extension of God's love.

Whether you pitch in to help a friend, surprise a stranger by buying lunch or bless the poor, when you are generous, you reflect the Father's heart. Today, tune in to the needs of others and discover the joy of generosity.

REFLECT In what ways am I generous—sharing my very best with others?

PRAY Generous God, I'm encouraged by the way You give—constantly, lavishly, perfectly. Even Your intentions are pure. No one can outdo You, and I want to be just like You! Benevolent. Considerate. Gracious. Help me to notice those whom I can bless today, and give me creative ways to display Your generosity.

DECLARE I am generous with others because God is generous with me.

ACT Out of God's love in your heart for someone, give generously to him or her today.

54 | CHEERFUL

> Everything seems to go wrong when you feel weak and depressed. But when you choose to be cheerful, every day will bring you more and more joy and fullness.
>
> Proverbs 15:15 TPT

Did you know that being cheerful is a choice? Even when things are going wrong, you can choose the attitude and actions you express.

It's time to treat discouragement and heaviness like a plague! We cannot afford to allow circumstances to dictate the way we feel. Yes, some really bad things happen in life that we need to process. But the moment we notice our peace and joy have slipped away, we need to run to the Lord and process with Him. Jesus said, "In the world you will have tribulation; but be of good cheer, I have overcome the world" (John 16:33 NKJV). The Holy Spirit is with us, reminding us of His presence and power, faithfully helping us to overcome. He blesses us with joy that contradicts our situations.

Being cheerful is a heart stance that can be seen on faces and heard in voices. It comes from the Spirit of joy living within you. Cheerfulness is a declaration of faith: "God loves me, and everything is going to work out for my good!"

Cheerfulness attracts more cheerfulness. A joyful heart helps keep you healthy and spreads God's joy wherever you go. You will discover strength when you choose to be cheerful.

REFLECT When I have chosen to be cheerful regardless of how I feel, what has been the result?

PRAY Father of Joy, I'm not as cheerful as I'd like to be. Sometimes life gets me down, and I stay too long in the miry pit of disillusionment and discouragement. Until I feel like being cheerful, thank You for the fruit of joy found in the Holy Spirit, who lives within me. I'm shaking off negativity and choosing to rejoice!

DECLARE I am full of the Spirit's joy, and I choose to be cheerful.

ACT Smile and do something cheerful, even if you feel silly or have to fake it. Then do it again.

55 | PERSEVERE

Consider it pure joy, my brothers and sisters, whenever you face trials of many kinds, because you know that the testing of your faith produces perseverance. Let perseverance finish its work so that you may be mature and complete, not lacking anything.

James 1:2–4 NIV

How is your faith currently being tested? Tests expose weaknesses, but God is ready to help you persevere. Every trial is an opportunity for greater maturity and victory.

Perseverance is like exercise for our spiritual muscles. We may falter under the weight of burdens, but when we trust the Lord, we rise stronger. Each time we face a trial and turn to God, He uses it for our good. He reveals Himself and proves His love, which increases our faith and matures us.

But what do you do if it seems as though God isn't showing up or coming through? You hang on! Even if the strands of your faith are wearing thin, you persist. Fuel your faith by grounding yourself in the Word, worship and biblical encouragement. Once the storm passes, you will realize how present God was during your difficult time.

The surprising end result of perseverance is no lack of anything. Wherever you lack, persevere. Perseverance is your path to maturity and complete satisfaction. So, don't give up! Let perseverance do its perfect work in your life.

REFLECT What activities provide me inner strength to persevere? Exercise, time alone, friends, worship, something else?

PRAY Strong and True Savior, You persevered to the end and overcame. By Your Spirit, I can do the same. I am joyful for the opportunity to persist through this trial. I know You will help me pass this test of faith. Holy Spirit, complete the work of persistence in my life so that I am conformed into Christ's image, fully mature and lacking nothing.

DECLARE The Holy Spirit gives me strength to persevere. When I persevere, I grow in maturity.

ACT Engage in an activity that gives you hope and strength to persevere.

But Mary kept all these things and pondered them
in her heart.

Luke 2:19 NKJV

When you have an encounter of such magnitude like
Mary did, or even if you just need to step back to gain
some clarity, the best thing you can do is ponder.

We love when God reveals truths we have not seen
before in His Word, encounters us with His presence
or awakens our hearts with dreams and visions. But are
we being faithful with these precious jewels and taking
time to ponder them?

Pondering—deeply considering the revelation He
imparts—is one way to show that we value what God
teaches. We can do this by studying the Scriptures He
highlights or journaling our experiences and what the
Holy Spirit speaks to our hearts. The more we pour
over the small truths He gives, the more they expand.
When we do as Mary did and keep these things close to
our hearts, God entrusts us with more.

If you receive truth from the Lord but do not respond
to it, you are what the Bible calls a "forgetful hearer" (see

James 1:25 NKJV). The Lord wants you to be a good steward of what He has entrusted to you. Pondering draws out His wisdom so you can walk in it.

Honor the Lord by pondering His truths.

REFLECT How has pondering a perplexing situation helped me in the past?

PRAY Patient Father, the revelations You give excite my heart! Forgive me for not always honoring them by spending time pondering them with You. I repent for the times I've rushed ahead, seeking something new when You have already given me so much to chew on. I will pay more attention and value the truths you give.

DECLARE The Holy Spirit releases perspective and peace as I ponder.

ACT Take time to reflect on a recent event that could use some pondering. Then talk it through with God or a trusted friend.

> Take full advantage of every day as you spend your
> life for his purposes.
>
> Ephesians 5:16 TPT

God has been good in your past, and God will be good
in your future. But God has something special for you
today, and being present keeps you alert to see it and
enjoy it.

All followers of Jesus hear His voice and catch
prophetic glimpses of His future plans. But we cannot
live in the future and neglect the present. We have
become desensitized to the present because we're
either looking ahead or dwelling on the past. We
must leave the past with God and trust Him with the
future.

We live in a fast-paced world filled with projects,
deadlines and a constant draw on our attention. Personal technology has exacerbated the problem of distraction. We allow it to interrupt a conversation with a
friend. While standing in line, we reach for the phone
instead of savoring a minute of silence or asking God if
He has set us up to talk to someone near us.

Every moment is unique and precious—an opportunity to tune in to the Father's heart and fellowship with the Holy Spirit. Find Him today in every situation and be present with those He has placed in front of you.

REFLECT What is something I can do to be more present with the Lord and with others?

PRAY Eternal God, I hear You speaking to me, encouraging me to slow down and pay attention. Teach me how to do this—how to cherish and take in everything this minute contains. With You as my Shepherd, I can be sure that You are leading me every moment of every day.

DECLARE I am intentionally present to take full advantage of what God is doing today.

ACT Deal with a distraction that is keeping you from being present in your relationship with God and others.

58 | HIDDEN

Behold, You desire truth in the inward parts, and in the hidden part You will make me to know wisdom. Create in me a clean heart, O God, and renew a steadfast spirit within me.

Psalm 51:6, 10 NKJV

God desires light and truth in places only you and He can see. He desires to commune with you in the hidden places and impart wisdom. But when your inward parts get clouded with sin, your spirit becomes unstable.

You will not hear the world talk much about "sin," or falling short of God's standard of righteousness. If you label anything as sin, you will be called out for being judgmental or prejudiced. If you question people's beliefs or actions, most likely they will feel attacked and remove you from their lives. You may also notice that behaviors hidden from the public eye years ago are now practiced in plain view. A person no longer needs to hide what the Bible calls sin. He or she can find a group that will not only approve of it but also celebrate it.

The Holy Spirit's role is to "convict the world of its sin, and of God's righteousness, and of the coming judgment" (John 16:8 NLT). Whether you are trying to hide something or proudly displaying it, when you sense the conviction of the Holy Spirit, ask Him to create in you a pure heart. And He will.

☀ **REFLECT** What is the Holy Spirit convicting me about?

☀ **PRAY** Lord Jesus, I confess I have sinned and ask You to forgive me. Wash me whiter than snow and create in me a clean heart. Spirit of God, renew a right spirit within me. Refine every thought, so each one rises to bless Your name. Instead of hiding my sins, I am now hidden with Christ and enjoy the refuge of Your hiding place.

☀ **DECLARE** Jesus meets me in hidden places and provides wisdom.

☀ **ACT** Consider how you might wisely bring something you have hidden into the light.

59 | VISION

When you see this, your heart will rejoice and you will flourish like grass.

Isaiah 66:14 NIV

Are you experiencing joy? Do you feel like you are flourishing? What you feast your eyes on has a direct effect on your faith and the way you experience life.

We all go through times when it feels as though we're walking in a fog. The enemy throws smokescreens in front of us, and we can't seem to find our way. But right here, in the muddied middle of doubt, fear or weariness, God directs our eyes back to Him. When we set our sights on Him, allowing our vision to adjust to the glory just on the other side of turmoil, it fuels our faith.

If all we see are problems, controversies and impossibilities, we are missing the bigger picture. God wants to give us fresh vision. We see the answer the moment we see Him. He is the answer to every difficulty. If we direct our attention to the truth, fear won't rule our lives, and heaviness won't find a place to land. It's hard to complain when all we see is glory.

Stop meditating on what is wrong or not working. The Holy Spirit will roll away the dark clouds, renew your hope and refresh your vision.

⁜ **REFLECT** If someone asked you, "What's your vision?" how would you respond?

⁜ **PRAY** Faithful One, I'm turning away from visions of defeat and unanswered prayer. You are waiting for me to come into agreement with You, so You can show Yourself faithful and strong. Instead of striving for solutions outside of Your grace, I set my eyes on You and rejoice in Your promises. Fill my sight with only You and Your lifegiving plans.

⁜ **DECLARE** God gives me fresh vision to see.

⁜ **ACT** Think about your past and present circumstances. What encouraging things do you see in your future with the Holy Spirit's guidance and strength?

60 | APPROACHABLE

Seek the Lord Yahweh when he makes himself approachable; call upon him when you sense he is near.

Isaiah 55:6 TPT

God makes Himself approachable. What can you do to follow His example?

This glorious One, who clothes Himself with light, stands with arms wide open. He loves you, listens to you, enjoys you and is wooing you to know Him more. He doesn't have bad days. He isn't angry with you, and He doesn't need a break from you. He is full of compassion and kindness. He formed you in His image and loves you deeply, which is why Jesus made a way for you to draw close.

It is easy to be kind to those we know and like. But are we approachable to those we don't know? What about a stranger standing in line next to us or a colleague who carries a distinct vibe that makes us uncomfortable? Do we avoid or hold at arm's length those kinds of people, or are we willing to approach them with Jesus' love? Will we let others approach us with questions, concerns or angry complaints?

Jesus invites everyone to seek Him and then accepts all who come to Him. When others seek you out, be approachable. This will draw them to the Spirit of God inside you, displaying the character of Christ.

REFLECT How approachable do others feel I am?

PRAY Approachable Father, I want to be like You—to be someone others trust and are drawn to, so I can be an example of Your kindness and acceptance. You don't agree with everything I say and do, yet You never disrespect me or push me away. You are humble and open. Help me to remember this when I'm around others today.

DECLARE I am approachable for those whom God wants to interact with me.

ACT Ask the Holy Spirit to show you something you can do to make yourself more approachable. Then act on what He says.

61 | MULTIPLY

Then God blessed them and said, "Be fruitful and multiply. Fill the earth and govern it."

Genesis 1:28 NLT

Everything that God plants grows . . . a lot! So why do you strive so hard to add when you can cooperate with the Spirit and see supernatural multiplication?

Creation was founded on the principle of multiplication. Within every living thing is a seed, which reproduces after itself. Left alone without pruning, nature overtakes everything around it. Grasses, plants and trees multiply effortlessly with only the sun, wind and rain.

But we humans strenuously labor just to gain a few more dollars to buy a few more possessions we hope will bring us joy. We remain faithful for decades but see only nominal fruit where we have sown sacrificially. But there are others who have sown and reaped abundantly by the Spirit. God has so much more in store for those who live by the Spirit and cooperate with His work by faith.

Adding more to do is not your answer when God wants to multiply. Observe the seed *God* has placed in your hand. Then plant it in faith and prayerfully care for it, expecting that His supernatural power will bountifully bless your harvest and multiply it. Do not just hope for normal growth; ask for exponential growth.

REFLECT What can I do differently to see greater multiplication in my life?

PRAY Miracle Worker, You multiply whatever the Father puts into Your hands. Show me what You have made available to me that You want to be fruitful and multiply. Help me move from adding things to my life to seeing exponential growth for Your Kingdom. Grant me the gift of faith to believe, step forward and govern what You have entrusted to me.

DECLARE God has blessed me to be fruitful and multiply.

ACT Do something personally or professionally to move from addition to multiplication.

62 | ANGELS

> God sends angels with special orders to protect
> you wherever you go, defending you from all harm.
>
> Psalm 91:11 TPT

Every day, God's angels are working on your behalf.
These protectors and messengers have special orders
from your heavenly Father to be with you throughout
your life. Are you aware of them?

Thank God for His angels! Both the Bible and history
record many human encounters with these heavenly
beings. Countless times they have come to our rescue,
whispered for us to change direction on a busy highway
to avoid an accident and brought comfort during loss
and strength to persevere. Though we rarely will see
them with our natural eyes, and we certainly don't worship them, they are a large part of our lives.

Just on the other side of this natural veil lies the
realm of the spirit of which we are a part. Every moment our thoughts, words and actions have ripple
effects—attracting blessings or giving way to the enemy's attacks. When we walk with an awareness of this
realm, setting our minds on things above, we begin to

notice the role angels play in our lives. And when we see the many ways God intervenes on our behalf, He becomes more real to us.

So today, be aware of these heavenly helpers who work with the Holy Spirit to guide and protect.

REFLECT When have you or someone you know encountered angelic assistance?

PRAY Lord Jesus, Commander of the Heavenly Host, throughout history Your angels have interacted with Your followers and those whom You are drawing to Yourself. Thank You for their ministry in my life and how they protect, encourage and reveal Your will. Dispatch Your angels to help fulfill Your Kingdom purposes happening around me, and help me cooperate with all You are doing.

DECLARE Angels minister to me and attend to my needs.

ACT Ask the Lord to dispatch His angels to assist with a cause dear to your heart.

63 | SPONTANEOUS

For the LORD is the one who shaped the mountains, stirs up the winds, and reveals his thoughts to mankind.

Amos 4:13 NLT

What are some of the ways God reveals His thoughts to you? Have you ever dismissed a thought that passed through your mind and then later in the day wished you had acted upon the inspirational nudge?

The Holy Spirit loves to speak to us. Though some have heard God audibly, most of us hear God's voice quietly within. We are one with Him, so His thoughts often get mistaken as our own. Spontaneous ideas that tiptoe through our minds may get overlooked, but the Lord is the frequent source of these random thoughts.

God doesn't yell or throw lightning bolts when He wants to get our attention. We are His children and His dwelling place, so He gently nudges us with a spontaneous idea. These random thoughts are easy to dismiss, but if we are intentional to lean into them, we will realize how much God is directing us.

The answer to your prayers, the wisdom you have been asking for or even a tip to improve your day often lands softly when you least expect it. Pay attention and obey the nudge. If it isn't a blatant sin and doesn't contradict God's Word, every spontaneous thought is worth prayerfully considering.

REFLECT What positive results have I seen when I have noticed a nudge from God and obeyed?

PRAY God of Creation, I am so encouraged to know that I hear You more than I realized! You are my faithful Shepherd, and You are teaching me to discern Your voice. Holy Spirit, help me not to ignore Your spontaneous thoughts and random ideas. I'll take each one to You and step out in faith.

DECLARE God sends spontaneous thoughts to direct my steps.

ACT Raise your awareness of the Spirit's nudges and respond to them in some way today.

64 | LIGHT

Send out your light and your truth; let them lead me; let them bring me to your holy hill and to your dwelling!

Psalm 43:3 ESV

When was the last time someone lied about you? Wouldn't it have been nice to have had someone come along to vindicate your cause, instead of getting stuck with the shame of unjust charges? God is someone who will vindicate you with His light and truth.

The beginning of this psalm shows the context for David's cry for God to send out His light. The false accusations he experienced had led him down the path of grief and oppression. Instead of trying to prove who was right or wrong, he cried out, "Vindicate me, O God, and defend my cause . . . deliver me!" (verse 1). David knew all would be seen in the light, and that this same light would guide him out of his depression into God's presence.

When you turn on the light in a room, darkness does not leave gradually. The moment light arrives, darkness flees. The light of Jesus is the same. There is never a question of its presence. Our God, the One who *is* light and truth, loves to penetrate every shadow of confusion or accusation.

The Holy Spirit is your Advocate. He will make things right as you choose to leave injustice in His hands and not take it into your own.

REFLECT What do I want to come into the light so others know the truth?

PRAY Brilliant One, shine the radiant light of Your presence and reveal the truth to dispel all lies that surround me. I put my reputation in Your hands. Vindicate my cause, Lord. I trust You to make things right. Illuminate my mind, refresh my soul and lead me toward Your holy dwelling place.

DECLARE God's light and truth lead me.

ACT Ask the Holy Spirit to shine His light in an area that needs His illumination, and then look to see what He reveals.

65 | FULL

But [Stephen], full of the Holy Spirit, gazed into heaven and saw the glory of God, and Jesus standing at the right hand of God.

Acts 7:55 ESV

Whatever has filled your soul will show up when you are under pressure. God wants you to be full of the Spirit, who will open your eyes to see the glory of God.

Not long before Stephen's unjust murder, church leaders had recognized him as a man "full of faith and of the Holy Spirit," and "full of grace and power, [who] was doing great wonders and signs among the people" (Acts 6:5, 8 ESV). At one point, when he was being fiercely accused by lying witnesses, the Bible says that "his face was like the face of an angel" (6:15 ESV).

These are signs of someone full of the Holy Spirit. To walk in the fullness of God, we must empty ourselves of ungodly things through confession and repentance. When we confess our sins and turn away from them, Jesus is faithful to forgive us, cleanse us and fill us with His Spirit (see 1 John 1:9).

You don't have to feel full to demonstrate the fruit or power of the Spirit. The Holy Spirit will provide what you need in that moment. You only need to invite the Holy Spirit to flow through you as a conduit of His grace.

REFLECT How full do you feel? Empty, partly full, overflowing?

PRAY Lord Jesus, I want to be full of Your Spirit. Remove what takes up space in my soul: accusations, arguments, carnal desires, unforgiveness, fear and lies. Let nothing steal my heart for You and get in the way of Your work in my life. Fill my heart and vision so I can see You in every person and every situation.

DECLARE I am full of the Holy Spirit.

ACT Ask the Holy Spirit to fill you up. Then follow the Spirit to pour out to someone else what He has given to you.

66 | ROYALTY

> Redeeming love crowns you as royalty.
>
> Song of Songs 7:5 TPT

How do you carry yourself? Do you hide in the background, do you feel less than others or do you walk with steady confidence, knowing you are royalty?

You are a co-heir with a powerful King who rules the Kingdom of heaven and earth. You are cherished by the majestic Creator. Because of Jesus' life, death and resurrection, you are seated with Him in heavenly places. The greatness of His might surges through your being by the power of the Holy Spirit. The glory of His love has made you into a new creation. Through the gift of redemption, the crown of salvation sits upon your head, and you have been entrusted with the authority of heaven.

Never forget who you are because of Him. Don't partner with shame, fear or intimidation. When you make a mistake, you are not kicked out of the Kingdom. The King draws you closer to His heart.

In meekness and confidence, proceed as if the King is by your side—because He is. You are not only God's child; you are His anointed ambassador, called to release His glory and carry His great name into all the world.

REFLECT How do I view myself? As a commoner or as royalty?

PRAY King of all kings, You forgave and cleansed me with Your blood and graciously gave me robes of righteousness. You are my King, and I loyally follow You to do the work of Your Kingdom. Help me represent You well on the earth. One day I will lay my crown before Your throne, but for now, I wear it with gratefulness.

DECLARE Jesus, the King, crowns me with royalty.

ACT Ask the Holy Spirit if you think too little or too much of yourself, and then ask Him to show you His perspective of who you are in Christ.

67 | RETURN

Return to the LORD your God, for you have stumbled because of your iniquity; take words with you, and return to the LORD. Say to Him, "Take away all iniquity; receive us graciously, for we will offer the sacrifices of our lips."

Hosea 14:1–2 NKJV

When sin—great or small—disconnects you from communion with the Holy Spirit, you can return to Him, and He will receive you graciously.

It is easy to understand how murder and idolatry separate people from God, but what about smaller issues? For those making their best effort to follow the teachings and example of Jesus, worry, impatience or impure motives may be more common for them to trip over. Regardless of what gets in the way of absolute allegiance to God, it is vital to address it and repent.

How do you respond when you stumble? Some people fall into deep regret or self-hatred. Others ignore that anything happened, blame others or make excuses. Jesus invites us to avoid unnecessary drama and return to Him.

To return is to turn or come back *again*. Built into the word *return* is the understanding that it will happen more than once. And Jesus welcomes us every time. When we return to the Lord with a humble and teachable spirit, He draws us close, cleanses us and restores the joy of our salvation.

There are many ways to respond when you stumble. The next time you stumble, hear the Spirit's call to return.

REFLECT What did you do the last time you stumbled? Regret, ignore, excuse, return?

PRAY Merciful Savior, I don't want anything to hinder my relationship with You. Holy Spirit, I'm not afraid of Your convicting love. Search me and show me if anything in my life is displeasing to You. I return to You with my whole heart. Thank You for receiving me today, and help me get back on track quickly.

DECLARE When I stumble, I quickly return to the Lord.

ACT The next time you stumble, return quickly.

68 | SEASONS

> To everything there is a season, a time for every purpose under heaven.
>
> Ecclesiastes 3:1 NKJV

From birth to death, life is full of seasons. God plants beauty in each season for you to discover and enjoy.

Have you noticed that in some stages of your life, the days feel long, but as you age, the years seem to pass more quickly? Yet God has a purpose for every season. Acts 17:26–27 says that God "determined appointed seasons, and the boundaries of [human] dwellings, that they should seek the Lord" (WEB). In short, the primary purpose for every season of your life, no matter where you live or what you are doing, is to seek the Lord.

God will make good out of everything you go through. Even when the enemy throws a punch and leaves you temporarily dazed, God turns it for your good. Nothing is wasted when you set your heart on heaven. Seasons of stillness are meant to be refreshing. Times of dryness are meant to stir your spiritual thirst. Even when the cold winds of winter blow, Jesus offers you a place in His warm embrace. And when you're running with Him in the heat of summer, the wind of the Spirit and rivers of living water cool you off.

God's faithfulness will keep you in every season.

REFLECT What is God primarily doing in this season of my life, and how is He prodding me to seek Him?

PRAY Unchanging Lord, You are with me in this season of life, and You will lead me to the next at the right time. Help me be present and discover Your treasures where I'm currently planted. Prepare me for change that is coming, but whether things change immediately or stay the same for longer than I'd like, I will keep my eyes on You.

DECLARE Every season of my life is full of God's presence and purpose.

ACT Talk to a trusted friend or your spouse about this season of life. Discuss how you can fully embrace and enjoy this season despite its challenges.

69 | PARTNERSHIP

You will bring God glory when you accept and welcome one another as partners, just as the Anointed One has fully accepted you and received you as his partner.

Romans 15:7 TPT

The Father, Son and Spirit are One God, partnering together perfectly. In the beginning, God realized it was not good to be alone, so He created a partner.

Whether it is the Holy Spirit, a spouse, a family member or a friend, God has meaningful partners for you in this life. God has also bestowed a great honor upon you—to be His partner and a companion for others. United, loving partnership within the family of God brings honor to Jesus and shows the world that God is real (see John 13:35 and 17:21–23).

What a privilege to partner with the Creator of the universe, the Savior of the world. You get to be His hands, feet and voice. In total dependence and complete allegiance, you and the Holy Spirit express God's character and care for others through your unique style. Then the Spirit connects you to others for larger reach and impact. When those connections come, rely on the Holy Spirit to help you accept others warmly.

Don't despise the small beginnings or fear the big assignments. The mighty Spirit of God partners with you to accomplish perfectly the plan of God. But you are also part of a larger Body, where working in harmony releases the presence of God.

REFLECT What project am I working on right now that could use a partner?

PRAY Mighty Spirit of God, I want to partner with You as You fill the earth with glory. Thank You for fully accepting me and welcoming me to partner with You. In return, I willingly and lovingly partner with those You send to me. By this, let all people know that I love You, love others and am Your disciple.

DECLARE Partnership with the Holy Spirit releases the glory of God.

ACT Reach out to partner with someone today on a small or large task.

70 | RAISED

If then you were raised with Christ, seek those things which are above, where Christ is, sitting at the right hand of God. Set your mind on things above, not on things on the earth.

Colossians 3:1–2 NKJV

You have been raised with Christ, who sits in authority in heaven, and He calls you to remain in that position in your mindset.

If you are a child in God's Kingdom, it follows that you seek the things that are in the Kingdom, not what is outside of it. True children of God do what their Father desires because they have had a change of heart and are no longer living for themselves (see John 8:43–44). Being entertained or entangled with the affairs of the earth is not becoming to citizens of heaven.

Citizens of heaven are called to release what they see and hear there. This is not difficult because we are with Christ, who is seated next to the Father. God wants us to live in the reality of His nearness—to live so close to Him that our words and actions reveal the expressions of His heart.

Your position in Christ will affect your perspective of the world. Those who have never been raised with Christ have not tasted or seen God, so they settle for less. You have been raised with Christ, so do not lower yourself to anything less than His best for you.

☼ **REFLECT** What is something that looks very different from a heavenly perspective than it does from an earthly one?

☼ **PRAY** Resurrected One, because I am raised with You, I seek a lifestyle of devotion and continual communion with You. Help me to respond to the gentle nudges of Your Spirit when I allow my attention to slip. Even when I'm busy, I will set my heart on You. I will carry the awareness of Your presence at all times.

☼ **DECLARE** I have been raised with Christ, so I live from that divine perspective.

☼ **ACT** The next time you find yourself settling for less than God's best, boldly and confidently declare your true position in Christ, seated with Him above.

71 | UNVEILED

All of us who have had that veil removed can see
and reflect the glory of the Lord. And the Lord—
who is the Spirit—makes us more and more like
him as we are changed into his glorious image.

2 Corinthians 3:18 NLT

When Jesus, through His life, death and resurrection,
removed the veil of separation between you and God,
He opened up a vibrant new world for you. Every day
you are invited to come face-to-face with Him to be
transformed into His image.

This Scripture points back to when the Israelites asked
Moses, their leader, to put a veil over his face because they
were afraid of the radiant shine that would appear after
he was in God's presence. But whenever Moses went to
speak with the Lord, he took off the veil until he returned
to interact with the people again (see Exodus 34:29–35).

Because of Jesus, we can now see and reflect God's
glory. In the same way couples often grow to look more
like each other over time, the more we look at Jesus,
the more we look like Him. We will reflect the nature of
what we see.

Living with an unveiled face means you are not hiding, ashamed or drowning in feelings of unworthiness. You run toward God, not away from Him, because you know you will be different after being with Him.

The more you stand face-to-face with Jesus, the more you will brightly reflect the glory of the Lord.

REFLECT In what ways do I reflect the glory of the Lord because I have looked at Him?

PRAY Glorious Jesus, thank You for granting me unrestricted access to You. I love being able to run into Your presence and talk to You without any hindrances to our communion. I want to stand in this place of clarity. With eyes fixed on You, take me from glory to glory and transform my life.

DECLARE With unveiled face, I approach God and am transformed into His image.

ACT Invest an extended period of time looking at Jesus in His Word and through worship and prayer. Notice how your time with Him affects what you reflect.

72 | FAVOR

Let the favor of the Lord our God be upon us, and
. . . establish the work of our hands!

Psalm 90:17 ESV

God's favor is God's blessing to accomplish God's purpose. You receive favor from God because you are a
child of God. This does not mean everything goes perfectly in your life, but you have the attention of a good
Father, who cares for you and works things out in your
ultimate favor.

Your attitude is different when you believe you
are highly favored. You carry yourself differently, unaf-
fected by temporary setbacks. You expect goodness
and mercy to follow you. You become like a magnet—
the light of His glory in you attracting blessings.

Favor takes many forms, which can include possessions, influence and authority. Favor makes connections
and carves a smooth path. When doors shut, better
ones open. But the purpose of favor is to make God
famous and attract others to the Spirit of God in you.
Psalm 67:1 (NLT) says, "May God be merciful and bless
us. May his face smile with favor on us." The next verse

of the psalm says why: "That your way may be known on earth, your saving power among all nations" (ESV).

God gives you favor because He loves to bless His children. But favor surrounds you and operates through you to glorify God and fulfill His will.

REFLECT What do I have in my life right now because of God's favor?

PRAY Heavenly Father, You favor me because I am Your precious child. I believe You are for me, so it doesn't matter what comes against me. I'm standing on Your Word, tethering it to my heart. You have shielded me with favor, so others will know that You are good. Holy Spirit, help me release Your favor in love to those around me.

DECLARE I am blessed and surrounded by God's favor.

ACT Extend favor to someone today in a way that will be a blessing for him or her.

Because Your lovingkindness is better than life, my lips shall praise You. Thus I will bless You while I live; I will lift up my hands in Your name.

Psalm 63:3–4 NKJV

God's lovingkindness is better than life itself and inspires an expression of exuberant praise for all who experience it.

God's lovingkindness is meant to be experienced. And when it is, it sparks a response of praise that fuels our lives. It is felt in the magnitude of salvation, the restoration of peace, the joy that defies trials and the bliss of unexpected glory, as He breathes upon our hearts. It is also shown through small kindnesses that come through the people God has set in our lives, such as a thoughtful gift, a word of encouragement, the comfort of a hug or a helping hand.

Everywhere we look, we see a continual representation of our Father's eternal goodness. As His lovingkindness soaks into our souls, it transforms us, and we joyfully walk in this fruit of the Spirit, as taught in Galatians 5:22–23. We become kind, as He is kind. God's generosity, compassion and thoughtfulness aren't dependent upon our behavior. He is good, simply because He is, and we are called to imitate Him.

Thank the Lord for His tender lovingkindness to you and acknowledge what He has done to others. Then bless the Lord by releasing His lovingkindness into the world.

REFLECT What displays of lovingkindness from God and others mean the most to me?

PRAY Loving Father, Your kindness led me to repentance, and Your kindness keeps my heart tender. From the moment I wake until I sleep, I taste and see that You are good. Help me show forth this kindness, so others will experience it and know You are on their side. Give me the grace to love others as You love them.

DECLARE God's lovingkindness is better than life, so I praise Him.

ACT Do an act of kindness today for a person who does not know you.

74 | RELEASE

> Cast all your anxiety on him because he cares
> for you.
>
> 1 Peter 5:7 NIV

When you cast your anxiety on God, you are throwing it
off your heart and onto His.

When you release your worries to God, the Holy
Spirit replaces them with peace and goes to work on
your behalf to work things out for your good. After you
cast your anxiety on Christ, do not go running after it
to take it back.

The reason you should cast your anxiety on God is
because it does not belong on you. If anxiety has been
in your life a long time, it can become a friend, or feel
like it is a part of who you are. But you are not a fearful, anxious person. You are a child of God filled with
the Holy Spirit, who gives you power, love and a sound
mind (see 2 Timothy 1:7).

It is time to let go of your anxiety—to step out from
under the dark cloud of oppression and embrace freedom. Joy and peace can be restored, no matter how
long they have been gone.

Process your emotions honestly with the Holy Spirit. He already knows how you feel. Release concern, stress, pain, fear . . . everything that is producing anxiety. Don't hold them for another moment.

☀ **REFLECT** What is a concern that is pulling on my thoughts and emotions right now?

☀ **PRAY** Caring Father, I trust You with my heart and offer You my worries. I throw myself into Your arms and cast far from me all anxiety and stress. In return, fill me with Your precious and peaceful Spirit. Restore to me the joy of my salvation. I am cherished, cared for and destined to walk with You in emotional wholeness.

☀ **DECLARE** I release my worries to Jesus, who cares for me.

☀ **ACT** As a symbolic act of releasing your anxiety to Jesus, write down your worries on a piece of paper and physically release it to God in some way for His attention and care.

75 | ABLAZE

> "I have come to set the earth on fire, and how I wish
> it were already ablaze with fiery passion for God!"
>
> Luke 12:49 TPT

Jesus longs for your heart to be continually ablaze with
fiery passion for God. He also wants your fire to light
the hearts of those around you.

Passion for the Lord transforms our lives. When we
are ablaze with love for Him, that fire becomes a guid-
ing light for every decision, thought and deed. It ignites
every conversation and act of kindness. It burns away
temptations, stress and complacency.

There is no faking this kind of love. Those blazing
with passion leave a trail of fire wherever they go. This
wildfire is started by the Lord and is fueled by our surrender. Each day, turning our eyes to Him stokes the
embers of our hearts and purifies our souls. And as we
yield ourselves completely, fiery passion consumes us,
enabling us to set fires everywhere we go.

God's holy fire in your life must be tended in order
to stay ablaze. If it seems your love for God has grown
dim, or has been overshadowed by sin or distraction,

the Holy Spirit will reignite your heart. All you have to do is ask, then fan the flames by spending time with the Lord and enjoying His presence.

REFLECT What God-given passion or excitement has waned, but I know God wants to set ablaze once again?

PRAY Holy Spirit, Fire of God, I want to remain close to the fire of Your presence so my heart never grows cold. I want to dwell in Your sacred flames and behold Your glory every day of my life. Come and blow Your fiery breath upon my soul. Purify, comfort and empower me. Set me ablaze so I will never be the same.

DECLARE My heart is ablaze with fiery passion for God.

ACT Led by the Holy Spirit, pray privately for another person whose heart God wants to set on fire. Then take an opportune moment to share your fire with that person.

76 | JOY

Though you have not seen him, you love him; and even though you do not see him now, you believe in him and are filled with an inexpressible and glorious joy.

1 Peter 1:8 NIV

Joy—extreme bliss, cheer, delight and happiness— permeates the atmosphere of heaven. The Source of this heavenly joy lives within you, and the Holy Spirit makes it available to infuse your atmosphere on earth.

It is easy to let your circumstances control your emotions. He invites you, however, to access joy regardless of what's happening and let it change your circumstances—or at a minimum, fuel other fruit of the Spirit needed to get through the situation.

Joy goes beyond a happy state of mind. Joy is a powerful, spiritual fruit produced by faith in Jesus, the love of the Father and the work of the Spirit. Joy heals our souls and delivers us out of the muddy pit of despair. Joy liberates us to express the freedom that comes from trusting God unreservedly.

Joy is also a choice, in the same way you choose other fruit of the Spirit such as love, patience or kindness. The best time to express joy is when you are feeling a depressing emotion longer than what is healthy. Choosing joy will launch you into breakthrough because it releases God's presence.

Today, look to the Holy Spirit for the joy you need. Let it free your soul and catapult you into victory.

REFLECT How do I view joy—as a superfluous, nice-to-have feeling, or as a fruit of the Spirit that is always available to me?

PRAY Father of Joy, in Your presence is fullness of joy, not just a little bit. You anointed Jesus with the oil of joy more than any of His companions. Fill me with Your Spirit and nurture in me the fruit of joy. Let shouts of joy and victory resound in my life because You have done mighty things. My hope and my joy is in You!

DECLARE The hopeful joy of the Holy Spirit fills me.

ACT Express joy extravagantly in some way today.

"Be still, and know that I am God!"

Psalm 46:10 NLT

Young children sometimes receive a "time-out" to help them gain perspective and get their behavior back on track. Your loving heavenly Father will also at times invite you to pause, be still and remember He is Almighty God.

The writer of Psalm 46 detailed many things that can occupy our attention: times of trouble, earthquakes, wars, chaos in the nations and crumbling kingdoms. In the middle of the madness, God exclaims, "Be still, and know that I am God!" And so that we can calm ourselves and remain in peace, He reassures us that the "LORD of Heaven's Armies is here among us; the God of Israel is our fortress" (verse 11).

What is going on around us often gets our attention more than who is within us. The Holy Spirit dwells within us, but how often do we pause to become aware of Him? The Spirit is eager to comfort, guide and strengthen, but we neglect one of our greatest blessings if we are not intentionally tuning in to His active presence.

In conversations, pause. In decision making, goal setting and creating to-do lists, pause. Fellowship with the Spirit and enjoy the wonders He has for you each day.

REFLECT What kind of activities help me pause to gain perspective and realign my day with what I value most?

PRAY All-powerful God, You are my refuge and strength. You are high above all the earth and oversee the affairs of this world. In the middle of chaos, You invite me to be still and know You are God. So I pause, quiet myself and tune in to Your Spirit. Thank You that at any moment, I can pause and commune with You.

DECLARE When I pause with the Spirit, I gain perspective and purpose.

ACT Set a few alarms for yourself throughout the day. When they go off, pause and find a place of peace so you can talk with the Holy Spirit about your day.

As far as the east is from the west, so far has He removed our transgressions from us.

Psalm 103:12 NKJV

When God says He has removed your sins far from you, how far is *far*? God wants you to have this perspective about your sin after you have repented: Your sin is gone.

When you first came to Christ for salvation, by faith you received complete forgiveness, and the Holy Spirit brought you into His light. Your old identity vanished, and you became a new person (see 2 Corinthians 5:17). So why do you continue to recall things in your past that have long been forgiven?

Since the devil and his evil spirits could not stop your entrance into the Kingdom of God, now their strategy is to keep you ineffective in your service for God through reminders of past sins, shame and regret.

Your past sins don't need to get into the way again. God washes you and makes you whiter than snow (see Psalm 51:7). If you fall into sin, the Lord says, "He will again have compassion on us; he will tread our iniquities underfoot. You will cast all our sins into the depths of the sea" (Micah 7:19 ESV).

Once you've repented, your sins are the furthest thing from the Father's mind. Follow His example and cast them far from you, too.

☀ **REFLECT** What past sin or mistake continues to come up in my thoughts even though I know God has forgiven me?

☀ **PRAY** Jesus, my Savior, in Your great mercy You have removed every sin far from me. Despite what I've done, You say I am perfect, lacking nothing, because of salvation's gift. I want to see myself like You see me. Help me not to remember the sins You have chosen to obliterate. I am a new creation, held close to Your heart, because my sin is far-removed.

☀ **DECLARE** Jesus has removed my sins far from me.

☀ **ACT** If you have been unable to distance yourself from your past sins, reach out to talk with a spiritual leader or counselor.

79 | PATIENCE

> The Holy Spirit produces this kind of fruit in our lives: love, joy, peace, patience, kindness, goodness, faithfulness, gentleness, and self-control.
>
> Galatians 5:22–23 NLT

Have you ever prayed for patience? If you have, God probably answered by thrusting you into situations that called for you to put it into practice.

The demonstration of patience is proof of a deep, internal work of God's Spirit in you. It begins by yielding to the Lord in every circumstance and desiring His will above all else. When you resign yourself to His timing and are willing to see all things through His perspective, impatience loses its grip. Patience manifests when you trust He is working everything out for your good.

Impatience manifests when we are agitated or start to complain or argue. We get impatient because we think something is supposed to happen more quickly than it is. Expressions of impatience are attempts to speed things up, or sometimes just to vent in frustration. Galatians 6:9 encourages us, "Let's not be weary in doing good, for we will reap in due season, if we don't give up" (WEB).

Do not be discouraged if you find yourself being impatient. Quickly humble yourself and call out to the Holy Spirit for help. When you trust the Spirit's loving work to produce bountiful, godly fruit in your life, you are transformed from the inside out.

REFLECT Who has been the most patient with me in my life?

PRAY Holy Spirit, do a perfect work of patience in my life. I surrender my desire to get things done my way on my timetable. Help me to be completely humble and gentle, joyful in hope, patient in affliction and faithful in prayer. I want to be patient, bearing with others in love. I patiently trust You in all things.

DECLARE I exemplify patience by the power of the Spirit.

ACT Consider a person or situation that requires patience. Ask the Holy Spirit to give you insight, wisdom and grace to exercise the fruit of patience.

80 | UNCHANGING

Jesus Christ is the same yesterday, today, and forever.

Hebrews 13:8 NKJV

Yesterday, today, tomorrow and always, the Lord is the same. His character remains steady and strong.

Have you ever known someone for years who suddenly and surprisingly changed drastically for the worse? This will never happen with God. He is not fickle or moody. He is reliable. His love is eternal. His mercy is unfathomable. On every occasion, Jesus is faithful. When others disappoint, leave or break a promise, He comes as your Comforter and constant Friend.

The following verse in Hebrews explains why it is important for you to know that Jesus never changes: so you do not become "attracted by strange, new ideas. Your strength comes from God's grace, not from rules" (13:9 NLT). We must not fall into deception from the enemy, who daily slanders the character of God. The evil one also deceives people into false doctrines to condemn them to an eternity separated from God. But we can trust in the Holy Spirit to guide us into all truth.

Jesus Christ remains the same, but your understanding of Him will change as the Spirit reveals Himself to you. This will bring about change in your life as you become more like Christ.

REFLECT What aspect of God's character have I consistently experienced the most?

PRAY Unchanging One, thank You for being completely steady and reliable. I am in awe of Your consistency, mercy and grace. You are an unchanging source of strength, wisdom and peace. No matter what I face, I know Your love is fixed on me. Give me grace to be like You—a constant, faithful friend. You are my Helper. I will not fear.

DECLARE God's unchanging nature gives me stability and hope.

ACT Buy or create something that reminds you of an aspect of God's character that you want to remember so that it helps you in this season of your life. Put it somewhere prominent so you can see it regularly.

81 | AFFECTIONS

Above all, guard the affections of your heart, for they affect all that you are. Pay attention to the welfare of your innermost being, for from there flows the wellspring of life.

Proverbs 4:23 TPT

After you woke this morning, what was the first thought that came to mind, and in what direction did your affections first go?

Your affections are a big deal; they affect all you are. This is why—above everything else—God wants you to pay attention to what is going on inside your heart. Whether you woke up stressed about something or at rest in the Spirit's presence, every moment is an opportunity to put your affections where they belong.

Setting your affections on the Lord guides your heart. You dwell in God's presence and become stable under His protective shadow (see Psalm 91). Thoughts become clearer, more peaceful and in flow with the Holy Spirit. You become a wellspring of life that overflows and blesses others.

Psalm 86:11 (NIV) says, "Give me an undivided heart, that I may fear [honor] your name." When you sense your heart is divided or your affections are leading you astray, call out to the Holy Spirit. He will help unite your heart to honor the name of Jesus.

Your affections are important. God is jealous for them. Guard them so your innermost being is a wellspring of life to those around you.

☀ **REFLECT** Which of my affections needs to be guarded most?

☀ **PRAY** Loving Father, set my heart apart for only You. Help me guard it so that Your rivers of living water flow through it to bless those around me. Where my heart is divided, unite it in Christ. Holy Spirit, make my heart a wellspring of peace, hope and joy because it is consumed with thoughts of You.

☀ **DECLARE** My affections are set on Jesus and produce a wellspring of life.

☀ **ACT** Do something to guard one of your affections that currently needs additional care.

82 | CLARITY

> I hear the Lord saying, "I will stay close to you, instructing and guiding you along the pathway for your life. I will advise you along the way and lead you forth with my eyes as your guide."
>
> Psalm 32:8 TPT

God wants to give you clarity. It is His desire, even more than your own, that you would be free from the barrage of confusion and disillusionment.

No matter what has bewildered you—fear, anxiety or the complexity of what you're up against—God has the answer. It isn't found by brooding over a problem or begging Him to speak. One seldom discovers the treasures of His counsel in an atmosphere of turmoil. Clarity is found in the ambiance of surrender . . . in the nearness of His presence, looking into His eyes. In the simple yet profound act of trusting the Lord, He makes a divine exchange—your confusion for His clarity and peace.

God loves to speak to His children. He wants to give you understanding, but you won't connect with Him if you're stuck in your head. Surrender control, questions and concerns and find His beautiful face.

When you lock eyes with your Father and disengage with chaos, He will instruct, He will advise, He will guide and He will lead. In the quiet of your soul, you will hear His voice and find the clarity you need.

REFLECT What do I desire more clarity about currently?

PRAY Father God, Your presence centers me and helps me find my way. When I see Your face, Your eyes win me over and help me trust You. I hear You say, "I will stay close to you, and guide you in My paths." Thank You. I release the clutter and cares that have brought confusion. I trust Your love for me, and I let go so I can hear You clearly.

DECLARE The Spirit provides clarity to advise me along the way.

ACT Eliminate something that is creating clutter, distraction or confusion.

83 | VALUE

> Do nothing out of selfish ambition or vain conceit.
> Rather, in humility value others above yourselves,
> not looking to your own interests but each of you
> to the interests of the others.
>
> Philippians 2:3–4 NIV

When you value others above yourself, you are acting like Christ. When you look after another's interests before your own, Jesus is glorified through your humble sacrifice.

What is most important to you? Jesus wants you to set that aside and discover what is most important to someone else. God has promised to "supply every need of yours according to his riches in glory in Christ Jesus" (Philippians 4:19 WEB). If your needs are going to get met via the riches of heaven, why do you want to take things into your own hands and provide for yourself? God's way is to put others above yourself while He takes care of you.

The Scripture says to watch out for selfishness and pride, for they will disable your heart from wanting to put others first. If you see one of these ungodly motivators, quickly repent and get the focus off yourself. When you prioritize other people's interests above your own, they feel valued, known and loved.

Value what Jesus values: others. Direct your attention away from what's important to you and look out for the interests of others. When you do, you may find that God Himself has met your needs while your attention has been elsewhere.

REFLECT How can I put others ahead of my own interests today?

PRAY Lord Jesus, You are humble and kind. You know what interests me, and You look after my desires. Instead of looking at myself, I want to look to You and Your heart for others. Holy Spirit, help me value others above myself and look out for their interests before my own. I want to care for others like Jesus cares for me.

DECLARE I value others above myself and look out for their interests.

ACT Show another person value by looking out for his or her interests.

84 | TRUST

Trust in the LORD with all your heart, and lean not on your own understanding; in all your ways acknowledge Him, and He shall direct your paths.

Proverbs 3:5–6 NKJV

Never rely completely on your own understanding because it will not hold you up if you lean on it too hard. The Lord, however, is immovable and completely trustworthy.

Life will never stop handing you circumstances that are out of your control. What you do in these uncomfortable moments reveals how much you trust the Father. Trials are opportunities to see what is in your heart. These are the times when faith is purified, and you grow in character. When God is all you have to hold on to, you will experience the power of His might. He will show Himself strong on your behalf.

What do you lean on? Your ingenuity, money, status or wisdom? God recommends that you don't lean on any of that, but instead lean on Jesus and the work of the Spirit in your life.

But it is hard to lean on someone you do not know. Time with the Lord is necessary to grow trust. Until your time in fellowship with the Spirit exceeds your time trying to figure out a problem on your own, you will not trust the Lord consistently with your heart.

Try trusting God. It will strengthen your faith and deepen your relationship with Christ.

REFLECT What am I leaning on that could cause instability if it shifts?

PRAY Trustworthy God, I lean on You, not my own understanding. In everything I do, I want to know You and Your ways fully, fellowship with You and be led by You. You are faithful and completely trustworthy to show me Your paths of life. You have led me, held me and rescued me even when I didn't realize it. You have earned my trust.

DECLARE I trust the Lord completely; He guides every decision I make.

ACT Ask the Holy Spirit to bring understanding to any issue needing clarity. Also ask another trusted person's opinion.

85 | PROCESS

I long for more revelation of your truth, for I
love the light of your word as I meditate on your
decrees.

Psalm 119:48 TPT

Discovering the light of God in the Word incites a longing to know more about God. But seeking and finding is
a process that does not always yield immediate results.

Sometimes, in our excitement, we rush from one
encounter or revelation to the next, without understanding what God wants us to learn. Do we write down
the Scriptures He brings to our attention or ponder
what the Spirit reveals? Each dream in the night, brush
of His presence or whisper of God's voice is designed
to leave an imprint upon our hearts. He wants us to esteem His communication to us and press in for deeper
insight.

We may be grateful for all Christ has revealed, but
we also engage in the process of knowing more. The
Bible describes this tension: "Now we see things imper-
fectly, . . . but then we will see everything with perfect
clarity. All that I know now is partial and incomplete,

but then I will know everything completely" (1 Corinthians 13:12 NLT).

The Holy Spirit wants to trust you with hidden treasures in His Word. Mysteries are ready to be unveiled to those who esteem them as precious. Be patient with yourself. Press in and trust the process of the Spirit.

REFLECT Why do I fight the process and struggle while waiting for something important to come to pass?

PRAY Holy Spirit, my Teacher and Counselor, help me slow down when I haven't processed the magnificent truths You're teaching me now. I want to know You and esteem everything You say by pondering and processing with You. Help me to be faithful and diligent with every treasure You give.

DECLARE I engage wholeheartedly in the process of knowing God.

ACT Ensure there is a sound process in place, but trust the process and do not jump ahead of the Spirit's timing in your life.

86 | PRESS

Not that I have already attained, or am already per-
fected; but I press on, that I may lay hold of that for
which Christ Jesus has also laid hold of me.

Philippians 3:12 NKJV

God never wants you to give up, but instead press on
until you have completely laid hold of Christ's reward.

Every day is a journey. It's another opportunity to
grow in character, maturity and grace. Your relationship with Jesus takes you from one level of glory to the
next, but in order to lay hold of your blessings, you will
need to be determined. More than anything, you will
need to stir your passion for Him so you can endure
until the end.

Some may question your zeal, asking, "Why are you
pressing on so hard? Don't be so serious." Or possibly
you may get tired of the constant effort, and feel you
have done enough. Regardless of how long it takes to
see His promises come to pass, keep going!

Press in for wisdom. Press in to know Him. Keep
standing on His Word and rejoicing in your promised
breakthrough. If you grow weary, cry out to the Holy

Spirit for strength and press into the relationships He has given you. Surround yourself with people who will pray for you and stand by your side.

Don't stop pressing on. Christ Jesus laid hold of your life for a purpose, and that full purpose is worth discovering.

REFLECT In this season, what area of my life requires that I press on so I can lay hold of God's promises and purposes?

PRAY Persevering Savior, Your example and love sustain me when I feel like giving up. When I am weary and faint, You draw me to Your side and become my strength. The power of Your Spirit infuses me with courage and makes me bold. Thank You for Your patience and for reminding me who I am.

DECLARE I press on to lay hold of Christ and all He has for me.

ACT Determine one consistent action you can do in the coming weeks to help you "press on." Then do it.

87 | FORWARD

I focus on this one thing: Forgetting the past and looking forward to what lies ahead.

Philippians 3:13 NLT

What does the future hold? Does this question excite you or cause anxiety? It is time to let go of the past so you can experience the blessings that await.

God has glorious things in store for you. His hand is holding tightly to yours, leading you forward into a new season. Right in front of you, on the other side of letting go, His blessings await. But if you are stuck in the past, you may have a hard time believing it and moving forward.

Sometimes fear hinders us from stepping into God's best. Whether we've become discouraged or afraid of the unknown, or we don't want to leave what we have, ungodly mindsets can hinder forward momentum. To move on, we must leave our past in His hands. When we let go of questions, doubts and fear, God gives us something new in exchange: hope.

Sometimes releasing the past is painful. Sometimes the past was wonderful, and we fear the future won't hold the same joy. Whatever your situation, know that God shows Himself strong on behalf of those whose hearts are loyal to Him (see 2 Chronicles 16:9).

God wants to bless you, so forget what lies behind and run with Him into your glorious future.

REFLECT What am I really looking forward to in the days, weeks and years ahead?

PRAY Spirit of God, open my eyes to see the joys You have set before me—just on the other side of my surrender and trust. Be my Shepherd. Guide me so that I will not stumble. I let go of the past, in all of its joys and sorrows, and fix my gaze on You. I trust Your leadership and look forward to the rewards You have in store for me.

DECLARE I look forward to God's continued faithfulness in my life.

ACT Make a list and share with someone what you are looking forward to in the coming weeks, months and years.

> But you are a chosen people, a royal priesthood, a
> holy nation, God's special possession, that you may
> declare the praises of him who called you out of
> darkness into his wonderful light.
>
> 1 Peter 2:9 NIV

You have been chosen by the God of the universe, and
you have a purpose and a destiny.

No matter if you presently have a lower social status
or if you have an impressive title, your worth is not
marked by what you have or have not accomplished.
The precious blood of Jesus has declared your signifi-
cance and sealed your value.

God wants you to find your identity and worth in
Him. You are a part of God's chosen people, those
who minister to Him and represent His Kingdom in the
earth. You are His special possession, and He has taken
you out of darkness into His marvelous light. Does this
make you want to praise Him?

All you are and ever hope to be is a gift from your
Father, and He wants you to accept it. Set your heart
on Him and remember the price He paid to be with you

for eternity. You are His beloved, your life matters and you have His full attention today.

Lift your eyes to the Father, who has chosen you. If you look closely, you will see your reflection in His eyes. His love is set upon you and has given meaning to your life.

REFLECT Why do I think God chose me, and what is something I believe He has chosen just for me to do?

PRAY Merciful Father, show me why You have chosen me. Your love is amazing and overwhelms my heart. To know that You call me Your beloved fills me with hope and purpose. Give me the grace to live for You without reservation. I leave behind everything that doesn't reflect Your beauty, remembering that You have chosen to shine through me.

DECLARE I am God's chosen one, set apart and called into His wonderful light.

ACT Acknowledge that God has chosen you for a reason. In any way you have abdicated a responsibility that God gave to you, step back into it with purpose and the Spirit's power.

89 | SEATED

And God raised us up with Christ and seated us
with him in the heavenly realms in Christ Jesus.

Ephesians 2:6 NIV

When you are seated, you are not running around trying to make things happen. You are at rest and confident in your position.

The Bible teaches a great mystery: You were united
with Christ in His death, and so you were raised to life
as He was (see Romans 6:5). Spiritually, you ascended
to heaven with Christ, and now you not only occupy
space on earth, but you are also seated with Christ in
heavenly realms. You are a vessel filled with God's Spirit,
entrusted with His glory and called to rule and reign
with Him from this heavenly position of advantage and
authority.

Living in this understanding gives you confidence.
Striving is a thing of the past. You only need to strive to
enter His rest (see Hebrews 4:11). The place of rest is
sitting with Christ in heavenly places, believing in Him
and doing what You see the Father doing. Your position
with Christ in heaven is supposed to direct Your work

on this earth. All work takes effort, but work directed from heaven is blessed and empowered by the Spirit.

Stay seated with Christ. Don't get up and try to find a better spot. You are with Christ and have all you need.

REFLECT What does being seated in heavenly realms look like, and what are its implications for my everyday life?

PRAY Father God, thank You for seating me with Christ in heavenly realms. I am grateful for the wealth of Your grace and kindness. Holy Spirit, remind me that I am called to reign with Christ from a place of rest. I am a citizen of heaven, invited to live in the heights of Your glory and to release it on the earth.

DECLARE I am seated with Christ in heavenly places and live my life from that position.

ACT Look at a situation you are struggling with from your seated position in heavenly places. Act based on the new perspective you have gained.

90 | KEEP

Now to Him who is able to keep you from stumbling, and to present you faultless before the presence of His glory with exceeding joy.

Jude 1:24 NKJV

Jesus is looking forward to presenting you before His Father with exceeding joy! He not only has the power to *save* you, but He also has the power to *keep* you.

Some people live a brash, godless life and eventually come to Christ with a dramatic turn from darkness to light. This demonstrates Christ's power to save from sin. Others grow up knowing God, choose early to follow Him and never experience a season of reckless rebellion. This demonstrates Christ's power to save since none are righteous and all require salvation, but it also demonstrates Christ's power to keep a person from evil.

God's power to keep you is just as strong as His power to save you. You have an enemy that prowls around seeking whom he may devour. You need Someone to keep you on the narrow path, and you can trust the Holy Spirit, who is both able and willing to keep you from stumbling.

May God bless you, keep you, make His face shine upon you and be gracious unto you. May He also give His angels charge over you as you step into your future without fear, knowing the One who keeps you is faithful. With exceeding joy, Jesus will present you to the Father, faultless.

REFLECT In what area do I most want God to keep me from stumbling?

PRAY Lord God, thank You for Your unfathomable love that has saved me, has guided me and is now keeping me from stumbling. I look forward to standing before Your presence faultless. I yield to Your purifying work in my life because I know it will produce good fruit that will last. I trust in Your love and leadership.

DECLARE The Spirit keeps me from stumbling and will present me faultless before Christ.

ACT Picture yourself thirty years older, looking back on your life. Write a letter to your younger self detailing how God has kept you from stumbling.

SPECIAL INVITATION

As you read this book, you may have realized that you want to go deeper in your relationship with God, or that you have yet to welcome Jesus into your life and follow Him as King.

In the beginning, God created the world, and everything was good (see Genesis 1–2). But after the first humans disobeyed God, sin entered the world, which separated us from God and brought eternal death (see Genesis 3; Romans 3:23; 5:12; 6:23).

The good news is that "God so loved the world, that he gave his only Son [Jesus], that whoever believes in him should not perish but have eternal life" (John 3:16 ESV). Jesus came to earth, lived a sinless life and was crucified, receiving the punishment for our sins. He rose from the dead, defeating sin and death, and will return as King.

Will you receive Jesus as your Lord and Savior? Share your heart with God in this prayer: *Jesus, I no longer want to do things my way, and I choose to follow You as my Lord. Forgive me and fill me with Your Holy Spirit to live for You every day.*

TO DISCOVER RESOURCES TO HELP YOU GROW IN YOUR FAITH, VISIT

- Bible.com or the YouVersion Bible app
- Messengerx.com or the MessengerX app
- Faithful.co or the Faithful app
- Chosenbooks.com